BRECKLAND

BRECKLAND

OLIVE COOK

The country is the real thing, the substantial
thing, the eternal thing; it is the thing to
watch over and care for and be loyal to;
institutions are extraneous to it, they are its
mere clothing, and clothing can wear out,
become ragged, cease to be comfortable,
cease to protect the body from winter,
disease and death.

MARK TWAIN

ROBERT HALE · LONDON

Robert Hale Ltd
Clerkenwell House
Clerkenwell Green
London EC1

PRINTED IN GREAT BRITAIN BY
LOWE AND BRYDONE PRINTERS LTD, THETFORD, NORFOLK

CONTENTS

ILLUSTRATIONS

vii

ILLUSTRATIONS

The Little Ouse at Brandon

Cottages in Magdalen Street, Thetford

The Wesleyan Chapel, Eriswell

Oxburgh Hall

ACKNOWLEDGMENT
*The above illustrations are reproduced from photographs
by Edwin Smith*

PREFACE

BRECKLAND appeared almost a quarter of a century ago and my first reaction on rereading it after all those years was to shrink from the alien self I encountered in its pages, to deplore my youthful concentration on feeling at the expense of fact, and to be appalled by faults and omissions due to inadequate research. It seemed that nothing but a fresh start could repair the imperfections of the book and at the same time give some account of the great changes which have overtaken both writer and subject. A closer look did, however, suggest a single possible justification for bringing out another edition of the original text: it does manage to communicate something of the unique character and atmosphere of the region; and perhaps there is something to be said after all for reviving the record of certain personal experiences of a particular countryside which, though still strongly individual, can no longer, owing to the growth of population, the spread of industry and above all universal car ownership, be enjoyed with quite the same spirit of adventure and abandon. I have tried to improve the reliability of the book by putting right the most obvious of the factual errors in its pages, by pointing very briefly to some of the shortcomings I most regret, and by indicating the kind of developments which during the past two decades have metamorphozed this part of England no less than the rest of the country.

During the time I spent in Breckland in the fifties, when I travelled on foot or on a bicycle, I was dismayed by the intrusion of military traffic into the little towns of Thetford and Brandon and into the villages which had the misfortune to lie near the camps and aerodromes of Mildenhall and Lakenheath. Since then the U.S. airbase at Lakenheath has become one of the largest in Britain, taking up eleven thousand acres of Breckland. Yet its effect on roads and villages is no greater than the visual and aural devastation wrought by the increase in the volume of road transport, both private and public. It

has annihilated much of the solitude and natural life of warren
and forest, fostered the ugly growth of suburban sprawl and
industry and revolutionized the pattern of town and village
life. In Breckland as elsewhere the supermarket has encroached
upon the village shop, the pub has been given a face-lift,
children travel by bus to new schools and a car stands outside
nearly every council house and cottage. Even where innovation
has taken place relatively gently, as at East Harling, a comparison of the present village, where the little market square is
now a concreted car park, with that described in this book
shows the unmistakable signs of development stemming not
from factors within the village and its rural setting, but from
policies and attitudes of alien urban origin. An analysis of the
change in life styles and in the structure of society in Breckland
would be of particular interest, including as it would have to
do the impact of the considerable American population which
must be of much greater significance now than it appeared to
the casual eye of the writer in 1956. But this is clearly not the
place to embark on so vast a subject. I can only touch briefly
upon the visual repercussions of that change.

A few anachronistic and nostalgic survivals, visual if often
nothing more, of the old relationship between 'big house'
and village can still be found in Breckland. Hillborough
remains a delightful example and Euston, where the wooded
park yet displays one of the most inspired of Capability
Brown's transformations, continues to bear witness to an
almost vanished way of life. Elveden has now been partly
converted to workmen's flats, but its actual image is unaltered.
But the former amazing, time-stopping tranquillity of Kilverstone has been rudely assailed by tourist attractions—a wild
life park, a Latin-American zoo, a miniature horse stud, a
café, a gift shop and, most disquieting of all, a 'pet-patting
area'. The fate of the noble, romantic park of Weeting and its
decaying hall is as typical. The great house, the thatched
cottages of former tenants, the magnificent chestnuts and
beeches and undulating expanses of turf have given way to
a small town of mean bungalows. The Georgian mansion and
classical mausoleum of Brandon Park have been allowed to
disintegrate while the public walk and picnic and leave litter

in its woods and on its lawns.

Between Lakenheath and Brandon the heath is disfigured by row upon row of identical box-like dwelling. The pastoral charm of the river, mill and inn at Barton Mills has been irreparably ruined by concrete, housing and heavy main-road traffic. Thetford, now bypassed, has been restored to something of its former quiet, and in White Hart Street and King Street the visitor can enjoy more of the atmosphere of the leisurely, sleepy little spa of the early nineteenth century than I ever could in my youth. But alas several of the most expressive streets of flint cottages have been demolished to make way for a featureless shopping precinct, while yet another block of shops and offices rises by the river in Bridge Street near the much enlarged Bell Hotel on a site once graced by unpretentious flint and yellow brick terrace houses. The upper storey of the concrete structure exhibits a series of huge, diagonally set precast flint panels, a pathetic allusion to local tradition. The imaginative poverty and the incongruity of the modern enterprise are underlined by the existence a few miles away at Feltwell of a remarkable set of medieval flint panels. The village boasts two exceptional churches, both of which were most unjustifiably overlooked in the earlier edition of this book. St Mary is conspicuous for its rich, buttressed tower rising to an openwork parapet and flickering pinnacles, but it is St Nicholas which rivets the eye. Its round tower has almost entirely crumbled, its chancel too has gone, but from its high hill-top site the short, lofty nave of pale, lustrous flint boldly flaunts a row of large flushwork panels, a vividly arresting display, seen from afar, of symbolic designs and diapers like the optic devices of Bridget Riley.

On the outskirts of Thetford new housing has invaded the very monastic ruins, and along the bypass huge industrial estates have mushroomed, covering many more acres than old Thetford. An attempt here and there to create the sweet confusion of a true cottage garden where cabbages, runner-beans, onions, parsley and gooseberry bushes mingle with roses, turk's cap lilies, phlox, stocks, lavender and southern-wood, only accentuates the bleak uniformity of the houses and the Vulgarity of the hybrid and floribunda roses and ornamental cherries planted in most of the little gardens that have not been altogether neglected.

Brandon is similarly if not as extensively defaced. The approach to the town on the Thetford road is through industrial sites among which a few twisted pines recall the dramatic, primeval aspect of the scene in the fifties. A big estate of bungalows and G.L.C. 'overspill' estates conflict with the flint cottages which still stand, and giant concrete lamp standards of the gallows type ruin the proportions of the broad main street. The name of one of the developments, Warren Close, recalls the former vast rabbit warrens of the Brandon landscape and the special association of the town through its felt hat and fur factory with the most fecund inhabitant of Breckland. The effects of myxomatosis were already becoming apparent when this book was first published. The cony is now all but extinct in the region, Lingwood's factory is no more than a memory and it is only in place names that this once ubiquitous creature and with it the warrener's profession are still celebrated. An even more regrettable change in Brandon itself is the departure of the knappers from the Flint Knappers' Arms. The names of the pub, of the new estate, Knappers' Way, and of the town sign showing knappers at work are the only reminders of Brandon's ancient industry, although flint-knapping does go on now and then in cottages in the area.

While ruin still plays a part in the distinctive Breckland landscape, a number of formerly conspicuously romantic ruins have been so tidied as to have become quite prosaic. The crashed tower of Foulden has been removed after a lapse of two hundred years, the wild motte of Thetford Castle has been smoothed into a neat mound and the overgrown, suggestive remains of the castles at Castle Acre and Weeting are now the objects of scientific excavation. At Oxburgh, on the other hand, desolation has been replaced by a scene of idyllic charm in which the shattered church assumes much the same role as the artificial ruin of an eighteenth-century landscape garden. The Perpendicular north arcade still stands, its pale octagonal piers rising from the close-cut turf of the roofless nave. The Bedingfield Chapel has been completely freed from the tangle of weeds and saplings which half-obscured it at the time of my first visit and the amazing structures within it are fully revealed. It is now clear that this bizarre combination of Gothic and Renaissance forms comprises not one but two identical monuments. The fairground ebullience of the ornament is wonderfully set off by the verdour and serenity of the lawns and great trees, the pure Gothic fragments and the dream-like double image of the moated rust-red hall.

In general, owing to the mobility of all sections of the population, the extraordinary remoteness of the Breckland of my youth can rarely be experienced today. Parking and picnic places, some provided with picnic tables and waymarked walks, diminish if they do not always entirely extinguish the feeling of mystery and pioneer excitement once inspired by a walk across Cavenham or Weeting Heaths or through Emily's Wood. But Cavenham Heath, now a nature reserve, is still visually typical of Breckland before afforestation, and other landscapes do yet exist where the atmosphere of the region remains strong and strange enough to evoke an impassioned response. Such landscapes can be seen on East Wretham Heath with its two meres, Langmere and Ringmere, they abound in the Cockley Cley area and sustain the ancient character of Peddar's Way, especially where it crosses Brettenham, Roudham and Bridgeham Heaths and between Merton and East Wretham. Here the natural life of warren and forest can be richly enjoyed: crossbill, redstart, nightjar, stone curlew, harrier and shrike all breed here and red squirrels are not uncommon, and this despite the fact that because the Way passes beside the so-called Battle Area it sometimes resounds with the noise of the British and foreign troops who still train here. The Battle Area was created during the war years by the evacuation of five villages: Stanford, Lynford, Tottington, West Tofts and Buckenham Tofts. The passage of time has effaced the more brutal marks of the original appropriation and now the luxuriant and varied landscape of mixed woods, fir plantations, lakes (including Thompson Water), marshes, streams and heath wears a haunting and haunted character which seems only to be accentuated by the spasmodic military exercises. Derelict villages, deserted churches and numbers of largely unexcavated round barrows and flint mines deepen the sense of the past and by pointing to the transience of man's activities comfortingly announce the eventual fate of the concrete wastelands mentioned above. The theme is further illustrated, and with more detail, by the dilapidated Georgian stables at Buckenham Tofts, all that is preserved of the Hall; by Pugin's picturesque chancel at West Tofts and his transeptal chapel commemorating his patron's wife, Mrs Mary Elizabeth Sutton, who died in 1842; and by the flushwork inscriptions on the medieval tower celebrating name by name "all the beginers of the werk", wealthy merchants and landowners of whom this doomed building is the only memorial.

On Brettenham Heath close to Peddar's Way a small Romano-British site with typical grid plan testifies to the process of romanization which was intensified towards the end of the first century after the suppression of the Boudiccan revolt. It is probable that some of the defeated Iceni were set to work on the reconstruction of the road now known as Peddar's Way. These people who, because of their remarkable queen and their spirited stand first against the 9th Legion and then against Suetonius are more keenly present in our imagination than other prominent tribes of the period such as the Catuvellauni and the Trinovantes, have left traces all over Breckland and it is one of the defects of my book that they are not even mentioned. At the time of the landing of Claudius in A.D. 43 the Iceni inhabited Breckland and West Norfolk, though no site can yet be named as the definite seat of their monarchy. Their martial propensities and the high standards of their craftsmanship have been revealed in hoards of weapons, parts of chariots and finely enamelled pony-harness fittings with sinuous decoration, from at least five sites in Breckland— Elveden, Santon, Lakenheath, Icklingham and Ringstead. At Cockley Cley an Iceni village, which was destroyed when the Romans marched into Norfolk after the defeat of Boudicca, has been effectively reconstructed in a wide valley shadowed by dark pines and watered by a tributary of the Wissey, which broadens into a shallow lake in the luminous distance. With its moats, bubbling spring, wattle towers, look-out tree, dark snake pit into which captives were thrown to their death, with its huts, chariot house, long house and chief's house built like the house of Hunding in *The Valkyrie* round the trunk of an enormous trophy-hung tree, the village in its unravaged setting, half-hidden by willows, is a persuasive even if necessarily life-less replica, and would be still more convincing without the garish models of Iceni inhabitants encountered in the huts and houses.

Another interesting reconstruction which has taken place during recent years can be seen at West Stow. The remains of a large early Anglo-Saxon village were uncovered in 1973 and one of the huts has been re-erected on its original site, a little building with turf walls set on sleeper beams, with a thatched roof and the floor sunk into the sandy earth.

Although it is only in certain areas that the primitive charac-ter of Breckland emerges with its former sharp intensity, the topography of the region remains profoundly interesting. And some aspects of it deserve more thorough investigation than the cursory and too subjective glance they are accorded in the following pages. This applies most obviously to buildings and church furnishing, a field in which heightened awareness has been widely encouraged by Sir Nikolaus Pevsner's prodigious *Buildings of England* as well as by the decay and destruction of so much historic architecture. The sheer singularity of some of the more conspicuous Breckland monuments is a source of un-failing delight. The glorious east window of Mildenhall and the unusually large and impressive angels here and at Laken-heath and Sir Thomas Lovell's fantastic tomb achievement at East Harling have already made an appearance in this book. But the marvellous screen at Merton commands equal attention: its cusped roundels and ogees coil and undulate with such vigour that they seem like living thorns. The tombs in the Bedingfield chantry, the extraordinary manor house at Great Cressingham and the oriental extravaganza at Elveden have not been neglected, but the brilliantly inventive, crocketted oriel above the entrance of Hengrave was inexplicably passed over. As an instance of the unique Tudor synthesis of Gothic and Classic it rivals the Oxburgh tombs in originality and zest. Its shape, on plan, is that of a gigantic swelling trefoil corbelled out from the face of the wall in tier upon tier of multiform mouldings. And in the shelter of these flamboyant curves pairs of cherubs, either nude or dressed in Roman armour, support heraldic shields, the middle one displaying the Fishmongers' Arms and proclaiming the source of the builder's wealth, for Sir Thomas Kytson was a London merchant and a typical representative of the upstart nobility of his age. Another extraordinary gatehouse of the same period as Hengrave has been insufficiently emphasized in this book—that of West Stow. Three storeys high and narrowly confined, the brick design is pervaded by a strong oriental flavour. Squeezed between battlemented octagonal turrets and adorned with crocketted pepperpot domes and terminal terracotta figures, it is crowned at either end by a stepped gable surmounted by a figure raised on a niched, octagonal drum. Above the entrance arch stretches a broad, rich band of lozenge-shaped panels, each containing a quatrefoil. The uppermost storey of the long side elevations is surprisingly constructed of close-set timbers filled with brick nogging. Brick is also the material of an exotic little structure at Methwold, the gable end of the former vicarage. The bold composition, startling the village street, makes ingenious use of brick moulding. The principal feature, a central polygonal chimney stack is magnificently decorated with trefoil-headed blank arches, energetic lattice work and a vertical motif echoing the shape of the stepped gable.

The east front of Shadwell Park must not be forgotten, it so memorably exaggerates Victorian Gothic scorn of symmetry and passion for detail. It is a riot of corbelled turret, tower, oriel and gable with walls of flint and white brick and capitals and friezes entwined with naturalistic foliage populated by tiny humans and animals.

These examples of former omissions must suffice if I am not to embark on a new book. The present Breckland traveller will find the many remaining gaps splendidly filled by Pevsner and by the authorities listed in the Bibliography. If the book itself helps to stimulate enthusiasm for a fascinating region, if it encourages further exploration of its heaths, forests and villages and arouses concern for its future, which is part of the future of the whole of England, it has perhaps not been republished altogether in vain.

The Coach House, Saffron Walden, May 1979.

CHAPTER I

AT FIRST SIGHT

BRECKLAND and Breck are arresting, alien words, suggestive of
the stony, barren district they describe. It lies partly in Norfolk,
partly in Suffolk, some four hundred square miles which might
be roughly circumscribed by a line drawn through Narborough, Castle Acre, Watton, Attleborough, East Harling,
Garboldisham and Mildenhall. Within that line the characteristics of the country are curiously like those of the steppe-
lands of south-eastern Europe. For though it is bounded by
chalk and peat, Breckland itself is covered by a pall of sand of
varying thicknesses, where flowers, birds and insects flourish,
some of which are unknown in other parts of England, while
others are found only by the sea. Large, flint-strewn open fields
and derelict areas are typical of every parish. They are known
locally as Brecks and this induced the Thetford historian
and naturalist, William George Clarke, writing in the
Naturalist's Journal in 1894, to give the region the name of
Breckland.

At first sight the district is as harsh as its name. No stranger
travelling along the main road from Newmarket or from Bury
towards Thetford and Norwich can remain unaffected by the
extraordinary change which comes over the landscape as the
road enters Breckland. Coarse bracken invades rich grazing
meadows and eventually overpowers them; firs begin to mingle
with oak and elm; instead of hedges, rows of twisted pines
divide road and field. Wasteland littered with flints alternates
with vast tracts of heather, furze and bracken, brown lichen and
bent grass; and these give way to mile after mile of plantations
of Scotch, Corsican and Maritime pine. Not a flower brightens

I

their black, regular recesses; there is no sound but the crescendo of the wind through stiff branches; nothing breaks those uniform ranks of trees except a few scattered flint cottages with sparse, scrawny gardens or perhaps a tiny Edwardian hamlet of red brick, an over-restored church, a mulberry-coloured chapel and a neo-classic mansion. On a grey day those exposed heaths, those dark, unnaturally monotonous forests are not only forbidding, but sinister. The character of the scene appears to be not isolation but desolation and the casual visitor cannot be blamed who finds nothing to detain him, who experiences relief, indeed, at emerging once more into the pleasant, pastoral country of Norfolk or of Suffolk.

Even should some impulse urge him to leave the main road his unfavourable impression may only be reinforced. On a road as lonely as the one from Thetford to Croxton it is not unusual nowadays to meet with a seemingly endless, clanking procession of tanks, lorries and jeeps. Near Mildenhall, Brandon, Lakenheath, Ingham, Barnham and Wretham vast camps and aerodromes turn the landscape into a no-man's-land, the sad effect of all temporary, mushroom structures intensified here by their bleak surroundings. So much of Breckland is given over to military exercises or to afforestation that it appears vain to seek its original character.

Then, if nature is hostile, the works of man, as they first strike the eye, are no less so. East Anglia is famous for its churches, but though there are notable exceptions, most Breckland churches are small, stunted, either much restored or utterly decayed, while the whole district abounds in chapels and meeting-houses of every shape, size and material. There are two secular buildings which are works of art, Hengrave and Oxburgh, but many Breckland halls and mansions were built or rebuilt after fire or some other disaster within the last hundred years and have little claim on our attention but their size and history. The castles and monasteries which flourished in the Middle Ages have crumbled and the rough flints of their remains, some with their black, gleaming hearts exposed, give an air of finality to ruin which is never achieved by brick or large, more regular units of masonry. Flint is the principal building material of Breckland and its dark colour and uneven shape carry the austerity of the landscape into the little towns and impart an unyielding quality to the villages, many of which, like Santon or Wangford, lie far from the high road and consist of no more than two or three cottages and a few barns and outhouses.

Yet there is something in the atmosphere of these isolated villages which excites interest once the effort has been made to seek them out. The remote, foreign look of a place like East Harling immediately stirs the imagination. It has a wide, deserted market square, as stony as an open breck, and more like some unfrequented corner of France than anything English. On three sides it is surrounded by alien-looking cottages with ochre-coloured window frames, an ironmonger's store displaying farm implements and a smallish café. The main street crosses the fourth side and here two inns confront one another with naively-painted signs, one a fiery bull, the other a lean horse-head with rolling eye. One is well cared for, the other less so, and they inevitably recall Daudet's story of *Les deux Auberges*.

In time East Harling seems to belong far more to Daudet's period than our own, and that is true of nearly every Breckland town and village. Mr Michael Home, the Breckland novelist, deplores the changes brought by modern conditions to his native place and no one will deny that immense changes have come about; yet there are few parts of England where the sense of the past is stronger. At Hockham, Honington, Fakenham, West Stow, Troston, Euston, Icklingham All Saints and many other villages, the green of tussocky grass, the low cottages, the squat Victorian school-building and the chapels look as they must have done in the lives of our great-grandparents. And the contrast between hall and village which was part of the social fabric of the last century also lingers on in Breckland. Though at Weeting the hall is dismantled and the park despoiled by the huts of refugees and forest workers, though Bridgham has been turned into flats, Culford and Riddlesworth into schools and Hengrave has become a Catholic institution, the number of great Breckland estates which still preserve something of the old relationship between manor house and tenantry is surprising. I need only mention Euston, Elveden, Oxburgh, Shadwell and Kilverstone.

The inhabitants of Breckland sustain the impression created by their surroundings. They often complain that they have been invaded, that they are living under conditions which would scarcely be very different were an enemy army in occupation. American and British troops have taken possession of huge areas of Breckland; they have ravaged them almost as savagely as if a state of hostility actually obtained. Breckland housewives going to market to their nearest town are uncomfortably aware that their purses are neither so deep nor so well lined as those of the American women who have settled with their husbands in Mildenhall, Brandon, Thetford or Lakenheath. But these conditions have had no more than a superficial effect on the character of the people.

The Americans have introduced some startling innovations into the life of the towns in which they have been stationed; restaurants have sprung up with subdued lights and cocktail bars and plumply upholstered sofas; garlic, hitherto unknown in Breckland, is grown now in many a local garden. Nevertheless the waitresses in those smart new restaurants still cling to the East Anglian drawl and use expressions peculiar to Norfolk and Suffolk. "Now what'll yew be a goin' to eat together?" they will say and, to a soldier with an unmannerly dog, "Lawkamassy, take that there dog outside, dew that'll bark the place down." It is not uncommon in Breckland to meet older people who have never travelled farther than their nearest town and who cling to superstitions, old wives' tales and folk-lore. An almost toothless old man I met on Barnham Cross Common on a day of lashing wind and rain told me of a curse laid on Wamil Hall, Mildenhall. Whoever meddled with the house would die.

The wife of the present owner had tried to modernise the Hall and had been killed in a motoring accident. The old man had dreams of this woman and they always portended bad weather, he said. He also related the story of a local girl to whom he constantly referred to as "that dauntless mawther." She was renowned for her ability to lay ghosts and when the ghost of her master's mother appeared to her and said, "Mary be yew afeered o' me?" the girl answered, "No Mam. Oi've no call to be afeered of yew, for yew are dead and Oi'm alived," "which fair flummoxed that ole ghost". The dauntless maid extracted two bags of gold from the ghost, rid the house of the hauntings and, of course, married her master, "so arter all he got them bags of gold and he used to sticklick her whensoever he got drunk. And I dew think that there mawther desarved it for deceiving that ole ghost."

It is not unawareness of modern, town ways which preserves the use of dialect, relates an accident to a curse and ascribes supernatural powers to a maid who marries her master, nor is it indolence, but a strong feeling for individuality, the feeling which inspired a recent Mayoress of Thetford to forbid the use of motor-driven vehicles at funerals, the feeling which brought Nonconformity to many Breckland adherents and which perhaps accounts for the success of the American religious mission in Lakenheath and Mildenhall. It is an attitude of mind fostered by the landscape, not only by its lack of immediate charm, but by its powerfully primitive atmosphere, a characteristic so strong that change in thought or fashion loses all significance in its presence.

This primeval spirit finds conspicuous expression in the strangely contorted pines which are peculiar to Breckland. The pine was not actually introduced into the district until the early eighteenth century, yet because the tree was one of the first to grow in our land and was indeed common in the Jurassic Age one hundred and forty million years ago, it seems to be a symbol of antiquity. But it is above all the fantastic shapes of Breckland pines which rivet the attention. The scaly trunk of a giant tree at Thetford forms a loop about a foot across and looks as though it were the focal point of some religious rite. Modern lovers feel the power of the tree and plight their troth through the loop. I remember a lane near Oxburgh where rows of pines, their purple trunks spotted with brilliant orange where the bark had fallen away, writhe and twist, sometimes clasp one another and sometimes seem to change their positions, to lurch and gesticulate. Were it not for the mats of suckers chaining them to the earth and the ivy hampering their movements they would surely break into a wild measure. I saw them first against the apple-green sky of a hot evening. Behind them small, very pointed stooks of corn sloped in long lines towards another distant row of crooked pines. The spaces between the stooks were scarlet with poppies. It was a magic, if disquieting moment. Like the grim crags Wordsworth encountered by moonlight on the lake of Patterdale, the pines seemed to move with a purpose of their own, to be instinct with life terrifyingly remote from one's own.

It is during a storm that the essential quality of Breckland is most startlingly revealed. I was bicycling once across Gooderstone Warren on a sullen, heavy day. The heath was a livid yellow, much lighter than the intense sky. A dark, ragged cloud-bank lay over the distant village of Foulden and over Swaffham Forest. The foliage of a clump of immensely tall pines and oaks on my left wore that metallic, glittering aspect which presages a storm. Though it was early afternoon, night appeared to be falling, an unnatural night of utter silence. The birds, usually so clamorous here, larks, lapwings, stockdoves and pheasants, had all vanished; not a blade of grass, not a flower stirred and the scamper of a frightened rabbit only increased the sensation that the whole pulse of life had been momentarily arrested. I dismounted and the sound of my light shoes on the hard road seemed more disturbing, more presumptious than a raised voice in a sacred building. The menace of the scene and moment was completed by a deserted farmhouse on the edge of the warren. It was of flint, already falling into ruin. The rafters were exposed, doors and windows gaped, the chimney-stack had crumbled, bushes and weeds choked the entrance.

Suddenly a fierce, chilling gust of wind rushed over heath and forest. The trees below shivered and gasped like drowning men, the pines groaned as though rent by a giant hand, savage and frenzied. The lurid light on the warren failed, and with the second screeching onslaught of the wind came the roll of thunder and the splutter of big raindrops. I made for the shell of the house and took refuge in what had been the parlour. The ceiling was still almost entire but a paper patterned with pink stripes and roses peeled from the walls and flapped in the gale which tore through the paneless windows. The storm appeared to be directly overhead; lightning was incessant, and the wind howled over wood and warren before each majestic burst of thunder. It was as though the primeval spirit of the place had been unleashed by the wild weather. The sense of it lingered long after the sun came out again; it was stronger than the delicious scent of thyme in the storm-cleared air, more compelling than the sparkle of raindrops on all the roadside flowers.

Breckland is not only primitive in feeling: it has more links with the far-distant past than almost any other part of England. Relics of prehistory are everywhere to be found. Tracks which served prehistoric man as channels of communication have altered little since they first came into use; the flint tools and weapons fashioned by the Neolithic hunter can be picked up on path and warren, the mines from which the stones were prized are still to be seen on a heath near Weeting, and, strangest of all, the ancient craft of quarrying and shaping the flints, though now they are put to other purposes, is still practised unchanged at Brandon.

If the unexpected discovery of a flint arrowhead and a sudden awareness of the mystery and antiquity of Breckland do not altogether win over the unwilling admirer, he cannot but succumb to the spell of certain parts of the landscape which have escaped both afforestation and the War Office invasion. The grey day which seemed so hostile on the main road through Thetford Chase assumes a tender, poetic character on the shores of Fowlmere. This is one of several curious expanses of water in the district. Six swans make a ruffle of white on the cloudy mere. On the far side a pine-crowned eminence and the slate roof of Fowlmere farm show above a slope of clearest yellow-green. The thick belt of rushes and the dense growth of buckthorn, alders and willows on the westerly edge of the water are full of bird sounds which intensify the tranquillity of the scene. The quacking of mallard and gadwall, the clear, ringing call of the coot, the plaint of the peewit, the whit-whit of the little grebe mingle with the rustle of wings, with soft splashes and discreet wading movements. Two herons stand perfectly upright like thin, black sticks, in the shallows, then rise uncertainly and flap their way clumsily into the distance. A kingfisher darts along the water's edge like a shining blue ribbon drawn across the fringe of the reeds.

There is no more exhilarating spot in July than the sandy track which runs between South Pickenham and Cockley Cley. More lilac than yellow in the candid light of evening, it is eventually swallowed up by the low-lying, sombre mass of Swaffham Forest, but before it reaches the trees it dips through breezy, open country of splendid colour. The path itself is overgrown with pink and white striped sea-bindweed and extraordinarily large cinquefoil. A pale field of oats on the right is the only sign of cultivation; all the rest is open breck, covered with carpets of poppies, brilliant blue sheets of viper's bugloss, lady's bedstraw, rest harrow, knapweed, a crop of camomile so dense that it appears as if it must have been planted, and a vast, shining, undulating stretch of golden ragwort. And everywhere there are butterflies, Clouded Yellows, tawny High Brown Fritillaries, Vanessas among them, the Red and the White Admiral, butterflies of many species, fluttering, gliding, pirouetting on the knapweed heads and probing for the nectar of the bugloss.

After a few experiences of this kind, Breckland begins to

exert an irresistible fascination. Like other places, the fens of Cambridgeshire, for instance, which have no facile, obvious attractions, which have indeed a reputation for uncouthness, it richly rewards the effort to know and understand its strangeness. Upon nearer acquaintance the passion of W. G. Clarke for the Breckland heaths seems justified. It is easy to understand his reluctance to spend a night away from the warren and to appreciate the spirit which led him to shave with a prehistoric flint implement he found near Brandon.

Chapter II

FLINT

I. PREHISTORIC FLINTS

THE traveller on the road between Thetford and Mundford or on that between Brandon and Watton cannot fail to notice one of those Ministry of Works signs indicating the proximity of an Ancient Monument. The name of this monument, Grime's Graves, holds more than a hint of awesomeness; it breathes an antiquity greater than that of any architectural relic, and the direction marked by the finger-posts promises as much as the name. The posts stand at either end of a sandy track which crosses open brecks and the lonely plantation known as Snake Wood. The primitive looking mares' tails and rough bracken on either side of the track, the immense spikes of Aaron's rod growing strangely and stiffly against their dark, coniferous background are a fit prelude to an excursion into prehistory. Another sign points to a narrow opening in the trees. The path, only wide enough for the passage of a single person, is damp and sufficiently ill-lit to set the imagination so working upon the object of the expedition that it would not be altogether surprising if the hoary shape of the mythical Norse figure, Grima, the evil one, from whom the name Grime is thought to derive, were suddenly glimpsed among the trees.

Soon the plantation to the right of the path ends and a rolling slope of heathland comes into view. Next the path itself is terminated by a field gate opening on to a wide expanse of buoyant, thyme-scented turf, furze bushes and clumps of pines. Whatever spirits of ancient darkness haunt the wood they are instantly dispersed by the bracing air of this breeze-fretted spot. The swelling song of larks and often the shrill, mournful

10

"Willie Re-e-eve" of the stone-curlew, two pairs of which nest regularly on this warren, give such pleasure that for a moment Grime's Graves are forgotten.

Nothing of a monumental character strikes the eye and demands investigation. There are no massive earthworks or mounds, only a number of grassy depressions dotted about the heath and, not far from the gate, two small wooden huts side by side. It is odd in this isolated place to see emerging from the door of one of these structures a keeper dressed in the same livery as a National Gallery attendant. But his pointed, sunburnt face and broad Norfolk accent are reassuring. As a preliminary to the real excitements of the place he displays the contents of the second hut. Upon a shelf are arranged a number of flint implements: arrow heads, leaf shapes, axe heads and a hammer stone. Some of them are so finely worked they are translucent, and the flint varies in colour from palest butterscotch-yellow to glistening black, sometimes veined or spotted with white, brown, grey or green. There are also a number of waste flakes, such as were struck off in quantities as each tool was made and which are to be found everywhere on the heaths. The keeper is anxious to indicate the distinction between these flakes and the worked implements, so that no amateur archaeologist shall fall into error. He next shows a crude, cup-shaped chalk lamp and some whitened, broken objects with a texture like the bark of a tree. They are parts of the branching antlers of the red deer which were plentiful in the district some five thousand years ago. Such antlers were the picks used by Neolithic miners to prize flint from the pits, the sites of which are marked by the hollows noticed on the warren. It is an extraordinary sensation to clasp one of these picks, to feel its weight and its roughnesses and then to see the palm of one's hand white with chalk which was originally transferred to the pick from the hands of a workman who wielded it all those thousands of years ago.

Having made this moving contact with the remote past, the landscape outside the huts takes on a new significance. Those depressions, now seen to be very numerous, amounting, as Mr Mitchell says, to more than three hundred, are the relics of a long period, from about 10,000 to 600 B.C., when the district, now so desolate, was the centre of the flint-mining industry and one of the most densely inhabited parts of England. For centuries the true explanation of the concavities remained hidden. In 1586, in Camden's *Britannia*, they were referred to as "ancient fortifications called Grime's Graves, of which name the inhabitants can give no account"; in 1739 the Reverend F. Blomefield described the site as "a very curious Danish encampment", while over a hundred years later the Reverend C. R. Manning spoke of the remains of a "British village". In 1868 Canon William Greenwell, best known for his *British Barrows*, described as one of the dullest books ever written, and for having died in 1918 at the age of ninety-eight in full possession of his faculties, paid a visit to Grime's Graves and was determined to solve the mystery of their origin. It was a more formidable task than he had anticipated and it was only in April 1870 that he had the gratification of proving that the pits were not graves at all but mines from which Neolithic man had extracted the flint to make his tools. The pit Canon Greenwell excavated was found to be about thirty-nine feet deep and twenty-eight feet in diameter and it was filled with waste material, probably refuse from nearby dwellings, for it contained the bones of animals which had been broken open so that the marrow might be extracted, fragments of charcoal and pieces of pottery. The shaft had been cut through a bed of sand down to two bands of chalk and flint and at this depth galleries had been thrown out in various directions along the level of the stratum of flint. Some of these galleries were extensive and communicated with the galleries belonging to other shafts.

The roof of one of these galleries had collapsed and this occasioned Canon Greenwell's most spectacular discovery. When the debris was cleared it was seen that the flint had been worked out in three places, forming three hollows at the end of the gallery. In front of these hollows lay two picks, the tines pointing towards each other, and this led the Canon to suppose that they had been handled by a right- and left-handed man. The men had put down their tools at the end of a day's work ready to resume on the following morning. But during the night the gallery roof had fallen in and the picks had never been recovered. The picks, like those in the keeper's hut, were encrusted with chalk, in this case with the distinct impression of the workmen's fingers and the very print of their skin still upon them. It must have been a memorable experience to look on that piece of unfinished work with the tools just where their owners had left them on an evening three thousand years earlier.

Further excavations were made in 1914 by the Prehistoric Society of East Anglia, while from 1920 until 1939 work at Grime's Graves went on almost uninterruptedly. Two of the pits, dating from the latest phase of the Neolothic epoch, have been covered over and may be inspected by visitors. The first of these pits lies at some distance from the huts close to a number of depressions overgrown here and there with young birches and firs. The keeper unlocks and opens a trap door in the concrete top and discloses a ladder going down some forty feet into a dim, circular interior. Once the floor is reached the band of flint sought by the ancient miners can be seen shining through the chalk wall. Low openings, not more than three feet high, pierce the wall of the central chamber and give access to galleries leading away in all directions. There are ledges in the chalk inside the openings and upon them the miners rested the lamps they had cut from the chalk with their flint tools. Mr Mitchell puts candles on the ledges now to light the way for visitors. With heartening smile he will urge them to take a candle and, at the risk of covering their persons with chalk, to make their way along one of the low, dark galleries. The tunnels wind about, sometimes join one another, sometimes lead into another main shaft and sometimes, where exploration has not been completed, end abruptly against a solid block of waste matter. It is impossible to stand upright in the galleries and they induce a frightening sensation of claustrophobia as well as a feeling of wonder at what must have been the small stature of the men who worked in such conditions.

The second pit has far more magic. It has been roofed over with thick glass, such as admits the light from pavement openings to basement kitchens, and this glass has so encouraged the growth of delicate ferns and creepers all over the rough, sandy walls that the mine resembles a Gothic Revival grotto. At the bottom of the shaft there are seven gallery openings, but all are blocked within a few feet of the entrances and have apparently never been worked any farther. In the centre of the floor lies a pile of mossy stones and antler picks, left exactly as the excavators found them. Halfway up the shaft wall ferns frame a pretty little niche. When the pit was first opened this niche was occupied by the chalk-carved image of a pregnant woman gazing down at the pile of implements and at a chalk phallus. This particular pit yielded poor, faulty flint and the little shrine was probably set up to render it more fruitful. The presence of the image suggests that the Neolithic people, who made their way to Breckland from Spain, Portugal and Brittany, had brought with them some form of worship of the Mediterranean Earth Mother. Extremely naturalistic, incised representations of a feeding stag and the head of a hind, found on the flint floor of another pit, may also be connected with the magico-religious beliefs of the people.

Their spiritual life cannot be more than a matter of conjecture, but it is possible to reconstruct a rudimentary picture of their material conditions. The bones found amongst the waste matter show that Neolithic man kept and ate goats, sheep, horses, pigs, cows and also dogs. The dog bones are all those of very old animals; probably when they were no longer useful for hunting they were made to serve as food. Many skeletons of smaller, wild animals were discovered in the pits, which enlarge our conception of the Neolithic era. Among them were those of the shrew, the mole, the rabbit, the long-tailed fieldmouse, the field-vole and numerous skeletons of bats which had roosted in the galleries.

The Neolithic peoples were peace-loving, for they left no obviously warlike implements behind them. They were herdsmen, they kept domesticated animals, they had some knowledge of the potter's art and they knew something of spinning and weaving, for they dressed not only in animal skins but in the products of spindle and distaff. Among their personal ornaments were beads and pendants of jet, amber and bone. They buried their dead in a contracted posture and deposited a long, oval-shaped mound or barrow over the site. Such barrows are common sights in Breckland; among the most prominent may be mentioned those at Santon, Mildenhall, Croxton, Merton, Rushford, Weeting, Eriswell, Bodney, North Pickenham, Barnham, Thompson, Cockley Cley, Garboldisham and Mundford; and a great many more are mentioned by W. G. Clarke. Some of them have suggestive names such as Traveller's Hill, the Hill of Health. Howe Hill, Hangour Hill, Black Hill and Troston Mount.

It is apparent from the height of the galleries that Neolithic man was small. He had black hair and dark eyes, his skull was long, his face oval with high cheek-bones, an aquiline nose and a low forehead. Dim memories of these small, dark people gave rise later to a belief in fairies which persisted long in Breckland. They were thought to be swarthy, malicious creatures who haunted prehistoric burial-places. Their chief weapons, besides their magical powers, were flint arrow-heads which were known locally as elf-shots. Just as the iron-weaponed peoples who invaded Breckland from the Rhineland in about 500 B.C. were more than a match for the flint-armed inhabitants, so in the popular fantasy of a later age iron could always overcome the power of the fairies.

Many other ancient peoples, as I hope to point out later on, have left remembrances of themselves in Breckland, but none is so vividly present to the imagination as Neolithic man. Implements of even earlier periods are plentiful in Breckland, but they must be searched for in casual pits below the surface of the earth, Neolithic flints, on the contrary, lie exposed on cultivated fields as well as on the heaths, flung out by the activities of plough, mole and rabbit. It is possible to find well-worked implements in almost every parish where the land is still open, though they are, of course, small in number compared with the hundreds of thousands of flakes and chips which mark the site of every workshop. The Breckland flints in the fine museum collections at Thetford and Norwich were found in the parishes of Beechamwell, Cranwich, Hockham, Methwold, Mundford, Northwold, Rushford, Santon, Thetford, Weeting, Barnham, Cavenham, Eriswell, Fakenham, Icklingham, Lakenheath, Mildenhall and Wangford. According to the Brandon flint-knappers, one of the most fruitful parishes is Thompson, but I have never met with success there. The road between West Stow and Icklingham passes through a sandy, open heath which seems to be a profitable spot for searching, for here, not far from a swamp encircled by gigantic pines, I happened one lucky afternoon on three worked flints, a pointed tool and two arrow-heads. They were lying close to the road, so conspicuously placed that they caught my eye as I passed, though I was not consciously looking for flints at that moment. But my most exciting find, not because of its intrinsic worth, but because of the occasion, was on a strip of ploughed land along Santon Street, the track which runs parallel to the Little Ouse from the Thetford–Mundford road to Santon and Brandon. It had rained during the previous night and it is generally after the loose soil has been consolidated by moisture that the search for implements is most likely to be rewarded. It was a perfect summer evening of long shadows and light breezes. There was not a soul in sight and there was not a sound but the occasional movements of a rabbit and the loud hum of insects from the fringe of the Halfmoon Plantation. The sandy surface of the ploughed strip, where nothing appeared to be growing, not even a weed, was coffee-coloured still from the rain, and strewn with flints. I turned them all over eagerly. There did not seem

16

to be one worked implement among them. After searching intently for more than an hour I picked up what I took to be a pointed knife of translucent grey stone, but its shape proved on examination to be accidental; it was only a waste piece. Then a few minutes later I came on a button scraper, a lustrous little object exquisitely chipped. It was one of those magic, life-enhancing moments which, though rarely recorded, mean far more in the development of a human spirit than the facts of birth, marriage and death. It is difficult to convey exactly what I felt. My pleasure did not depend only on the discovery of the scraper, but it was as though all that moved me and had moved me at other times in the beauty of this place was concentrated in the instant when I took the flint into my hands. I was aware of the great antiquity of the lonely spot where I stood; and I felt as I clasped the implement that I had established contact with the hand that had fashioned it. I thought of all the uses to which flint had since been put in Breckland and how it had so largely shaped the character of the district. I glanced towards the round flint tower of Santon Church and remembered a day of deep snow when I had entered the solitary little building for respite from the intense cold. The meagre interior, shiny, varnished and Victorian, with a chancel roof of stars and rosettes, was faintly warmed by an antiquated oil stove placed at the end of the nave next to a tiny harmonium. Just as the air on this summer evening pulsated with the high, thin noise of insects, so the church on that winter day vibrated with a humming sound louder than the intermittent popping of the stove. Thousands of flies had sought refuge in the warmth, the floor was black with their corpses, while the living buzzed and hung in great, feebly moving clusters about the source of heat. This pitiful and surprising relic of summer brought back to my mind the July aspect of the landscape outside; I thought of a walk I had taken along the haling path of the Little Ouse, of the richness of the riverside flowers with the dazzle of butterflies and dragonflies above them. I particularly recalled the persistent hum of the insects which had accompanied and intensified the experience

2*   17

and which linked it now not only with the winter interior of Santon Church but with the present summer and the prehistoric tool I held in my hand.

2. MODERN FLINTKNAPPERS

Santon Street, where I found my scraper, follows the course of the river, passes Santon Downham, lying among trees on the far bank of the stream, and emerges in a huge timberyard on the outskirts of Brandon. The town stretches to the left of the river beyond an old-fashioned inn with the sign of the ram and over the modern bridge which, after years of hot debate, has replaced the picturesque seventeenth-century structure with its four irregular arches. The broad High Street slopes upwards almost imperceptibly from the water. Low flint houses, starkly set against the wide sky, a few quiet shops and an inn surmounted by the peeling, grimed effigy of a white hart make a singular impression of aloofness, of sharp, bracing denial of the cosiness and intimacy of the average English small country town. At right angles to the long main street, London Road passes Lingwood's hat and fur factory, an industry built up on the fecundity of Breckland rabbits. Here all attempt at town architecture ceases. Straggling, untidy gardens, chicken runs, a terrace or two of flint cottages, a few council houses give way to a waste of stony brecks and pines. Even the Church of St Peter does not relieve the desolation of the spot. It is much restored and contains little of interest apart from some mutilated bench-ends, conspicuous among them a cluster of fern fronds overshadowing a crude, headless figure with pipe-like arms in an attitude of prayer and with large plant forms growing on the front of her dress.

Yet Brandon, like Breckland itself, has the attraction of strangeness. There is an untamed look about its flintiness, a scent of heath and pine in its air which excites our more primitive instincts. Excitement is quickened by the hundreds of swifts whose scream haunts the town as they rake the eaves in their rapid flight, skim sidelong by the river or with a rush of wind swoop suddenly under the bridge. But more unusual than the atmosphere and aspect of the little town is its characteristic sound, the sound of clear, precise tapping which on every weekday of the year can be heard coming from the yard behind the Flintknappers' Arms, the public house at the corner of Thetford Road and High Street. It is a sound which has echoed, if not from exactly that spot, in that parish for thousands of years. It is the noise made by the flintknappers as they ply the trade of their Neolithic forebears, a trade followed nowhere else in England.

No one would guess from its appearance that the Flintknappers' Arms harboured anything so romantic as the survival of a prehistoric industry. It is a modern, mock Tudor house, built not of flint, but of alien brown bricks. The entrance to the yard is at the side. It is a small enclosure with two red-roofed sheds at one end, which provide shelter for the workers in inclement weather. Almost the entire space is taken up with a pile of beer-bottle crates and an enormous heap of flints towering as high as the shed roofs and nearly as high as a flint cottage behind the yard. Beside the huge, rugged shapes of the freshly quarried flints, the flints of the cottage wall, which ordinarily delight the eye with their irregularity, look as neat and even as rows of plain knitting. Some of the flints in the heap are startlingly black and white, others, from a pit near Grime's Graves, are golden. The quality of the black is dazzling, for it has not yet had time to grow dull from exposure to the air. Yet even more than their colour it is the outlandish forms of the flint which transfix the eye. The curving shapes that Henry Moore loves are among them; some are rounded as if they had been washed by the sea; others are knobbly and branched like tree trunks; some resemble great gulls with black beaks or with black feathers in their tails; and there are long-necked swans among them and heads of pure, white oxen with eyes like sloes; there is a cat with an ebony ring about its neck; an uprearing sea-lion keeps company with the gilded torso of an archaic Apollo and the proud, much-battered head and shoulders of a dark-haired ship's figurehead rise above a mass of triangular, spotted fish. Here and there a large spherical flint has split to disclose two jet roundels edged with a frill of white and marked in the centre with a white shape for all the world like a cameo profile of extraordinary size.

The flints are quarried by the same two men who afterwards knap them. Very often, in order to save time, the quarrying is done in the late evening by the light of lamps. The pits are near Brandon, on Lingheath Common, and another source of supply is a big open pit at Ashill, a village some miles away towards the north of Breckland. Great powdery cones of chalk have been flung up near the pit, striking a bizarre note in the landscape. They catch and reflect the light, changing from shining white to deepest indigo or sugar-pink with the passage of every cloud, and from a distance they look like phantom pyramids starting up from the brecks.

The method of procuring flints on Lingheath Common scarcely differs from that of the ancient miners except that deer antler picks are no longer used. A shaft is sunk, circular in form, gradually decreasing in size towards the bottom, and the descent is made by means of a series of alternating ledges placed at right angles. The flints are brought to the surface by hand without the aid of machinery of any kind.

The flints are conveyed by lorry to the Flintknappers' Arms. Then, sitting at the foot of the flint mountain, close to the wall of the yard, the two knappers begin work. They are stationed on either side of a juniper tree, Mr Drewery facing the yard, Mr Newton in a dark, shady corner between the tree, the wall and the back of an outhouse. Each man sits by a knee-high table embedded in the earth and surrounded by flakes, chips, quarters and halves of flints. White, chalky dust lies on their clothes and skin and all about them. It is because the dust penetrates their throats and lungs that the flintknappers prefer, whenever possible, to work in the open air. The shaping of the flints follows a strict routine. First, with thick leather pads tied to their left knees, the men take the huge pieces of rough flint in their hands and with short, skilful blows from a blunt hammer reduce them to four smaller units. This is known as quartering. Flaking follows next. For this a pointed hammer is used, and so fast and sure are the workmen's strokes that in a few moments the flints are reduced to a pile of chips of various sizes. Now comes the final and most dexterous process of all, knapping. With a thin, sharp hammer, which he wields with the precision and rapidity of a machine, the craftsman shapes and moulds the chips to the purposes for which they are intended.

The flints are for the most part destined for a strange, incongruous use. A few flints are made for ornamental work in the restoration of churches, and quartered and flaked flints, which have not undergone the final process of knapping, are sometimes prepared for building purposes, but the ancient trade is chiefly supported by the demand for gunflints from Siam and parts of South America, where old-fashioned flintlock guns are still favoured. Where hundreds of men once fashioned knives, battle-axes, spear-heads and arrow-heads, where their descendants shaped flints for churches and houses and adorned tower and porch with exquisite flower, plant and geometric forms of shining ebony, where, with a feverish sense of urgency, scores of Brandon knappers tapped out flints for the British muskets levelled at Napoleon's army, now only two men sit at work, producing flints for the natives of places far more remote from the current of English life than this lonely East Anglian town. Perhaps in a few years there may be no one to carry on this venerable trade, for none of the Brandon youths, Mr Drewery reports, shows a desire to learn it. Yet it is not long since Mr F. Snare, the predecessor of the present knappers, was lamenting the absence of apprentices in the same way and now the craft is in the hands of the most able practitioners. If he has a spare moment Mr Drewery will hammer out an arrow-head fit to place beside the work of any Neolithic artist, and if he is pleased with his visitor he will present him with a little dark, flint heart of his own knapping. His skill equals that of another native of Brandon who, a century ago, passed off as genuine prehistoric relics implements he had himself fashioned. He was known as Flint Jack and he was also an adept at manufacturing spurious fibulae, coins and seals, but in the pursuit of this occupation he came to grief and not even an appeal on his behalf by the editor of the *Reliquary*, who extolled Flint Jack's superior antiquarian knowledge, could save him. What finally became of him nobody knows, but it is certain that much of his handiwork still reposes undetected in museums and in private collections of Neolithic flints.

3. BRECKLAND CHURCHES

Though Breckland is the home of the flintknappers and has provided the material for some of the proudest East Anglian churches, no one would visit the district on account of its ecclesiastical architecture. One or two churches indeed offer experiences as rewarding as those of their better-known neighbours over the border. The fine Norman chancel arch of Lakenheath, and the roof angels, their faces mutilated by the Puritans, their wings curling like chrysanthemum petals, must move the most prosaic observer. The apsidal chancel of Cockley Cley; the richly decorated porch of Honington with its canopied niches and patterns of flint and freestone, the extraordinarily powerful rendering of the Virgin and St John in the fourteenth-century carving of the Crucifixion on the font of the same church; the reed-thatched roof and the interior of Icklingham All Saints, all blanched and drained of colour except for one blazing window, where fragments of saintly figures lean above pinnacled Gothic follies; all these are not soon forgotten. Yet with these and some other exceptions, which I shall recall later, Breckland is characterised by small, isolated, poverty-stricken churches, either far gone in decay or over-restored. They may not excite the enthusiasm of the art historian, but they are so deeply expressive of the atmosphere of the place that not one is wholly without interest.

I have already mentioned the wizened little church of Santon. It is typical of many another in Breckland. At Hargham, a lonely enough spot on the edge of the heaths of Hargham and Snetterton, the bell tower stands apart from the church and has been allowed to fall into ruin. A pretty quatrefoil opening surmounts a shapeless pile of masonry in which the former entrance, choked with bushes and ivy, can just be made out. The door of the tiny church opens straight upon the harmonium which accompanies the rare services held in the sparse, lamp-lit interior. Fir and pine envelope church and tower, the odour of decay is all around and a white cow grazes in the churchyard, which is separated from the adjoining field only by a low, broken wall. Croxton, though small, looks at first sight important. Its round tower supports an octagon and it rises imposingly above an abrupt bank and the village street. But in summer the churchyard is so overgrown that the tombstones are hidden and the porch is as difficult of access as the palace of the Sleeping Beauty. Swallows nest in the worm-eaten beams and at the sound of a stranger fly screaming through a gap in the rusty wire which covers the outer doors. Inside the air is chill, and floor, pews, even the altar, are littered with the droppings of bats. Signs of neglect greet the eye everywhere; the mats are threadbare, the hassocks are broken, the oil lamps are dirty. The only surviving work of art in this depressing interior is an early nineteenth-century tombstone to Thomas and Sarah Bailey let into the floor. It is decorated with a boldly carved relief of the Good Samaritan on a background of mason's boasting.

Croxton is untended and uninviting; it seems to have succumbed to the hostility of the surrounding heaths. South Pickenham, on the other hand, though even smaller, sits more easily in a landscape softened by the Wissey. Like Croxton it has a round tower with an octagonal belfry, like Croxton it stand high. But where one repels the other attracts. Croxton

flint shines dark and steely against the open sky; South Pickenham's rough, golden yellow walls and red nave-roof glow before a background of beeches. A Romanesque monster with a
kindly leer presides over the homely, whitewashed interior and
from the barn-like roof hang three chandeliers, coronets of thin
brass, supporting candles between bands of tiny crosses. The
festive spirit of the little church is further enhanced by a small
organ set near to the entrance and painted by some Flemish
master with scenes of the Nativity and the Adoration; and by
a rollicking design carved along the purlins of birds and cherubs
terminating in scrolls.

It is rare that these tiny Breckland churches offer much
aesthetic pleasure, but occasionally an insignificant exterior may
conceal a prize. This is the case with Wordwell, a solitary,
greatly restored, extremely unpretentious little building situated in an unspoilt and picturesque part of Breckland, not far
from West Stow. The landscape is delightfully irregular. Low
alder hedges separate the narrow road from turnip fields and
slopes of sand and flint. The red-gold sand undulates towards a
row of pines and the pink rectangle of a house and then, near
the church, changes to soft meadow grass running down to extensive woods and embracing a cream-washed Tudor farmhouse, flint outbuildings, grazing cattle and a flurry of speckled
hens. Opposite the church is the great prehistoric mound
known as the Hill of Health.

The south porch of the church looks like the entrance to a
congregational chapel of the mid-nineteenth century and no
one would suspect the richness of the inner opening. It is early
Norman work with a tympanum showing two barking dogs
on either side of a tree branching out into intricate strap-work.
On passing beneath it the interior, so small that it seats at the
most fifty people, looks at first excessively plain, for the eye
goes instinctively towards the chancel, which is modern and
without ornament. Then an arched recess opposite the entrance
attracts attention. It was once a north doorway but has now
been closed. The top of the recess is taken up with an outstand-

ing Romanesque carving. Two strange figures, whose bald
heads, small round eyes and schematic bodies recall the tiki of
the Oceanic peoples, stand on either side of a strap-work design; one raises both arms, the other clasps a ring. These enig-
matic beings glance towards the benches, which are so low as
almost to escape notice. But they well repay inspection. They
are covered with carvings of even greater variety and more
subtle artistry than such well-known works as the benches at
Kersey, Balsham or Blythburgh. The wood is of a red hue, and
shows no sign of decay. Among the bench-ends are dogs of all
breeds, a cat, a winged griffin, and a creature with the head of a
man with a most sorrowful expression, the legs of a bull, arms
terminating in foliage and a cap of leaves on his head. But the
friezes along the backs of the benches are still more arresting.
Among formalised patterns of plants and shields a snarling por-
cupine, a ferocious bull and a whole menagerie make their appearance; an agonised jester tries to burst from the enveloping
leaves but, alas, his body ends in a scroll which catches him fast
to the frieze, just as the branch which forms the tail of a monster
with a man's face, a cock's comb, wings and cloven feet, makes
him part of the patterned foliage.

The modest exterior of Northwold conceals one of the most
splendid Easter sepulchres in the country. It is of great size,
twelve feet high and nine feet wide, built as usual on the north
side of the choir. It is executed in clunch and surmounted by
three elaborate Perpendicular canopies. Upon the lower part
are carved the four Roman soldiers who kept guard over
Christ's tomb; they lie among trees in abandoned attitudes of
sleep. Above them the sepulchre is deeply recessed, while the
wall at the back is occupied by a series of cusped niches which
once contained images. In the eastern corner of the sepulchre is
the arched repository of the pyx, which with the host was
formerly left there from Good Friday until Easter morning,
when it was joyfully removed in token of the resurrection.

There are probably a greater number of drastically restored
churches in Breckland than in any other district of the same size.

They are the work of the Victorian squires whose interest in the church was stimulated by the zeal most of their tenants showed for the chapel. Mundford's pseudo-Rhenish tower dominates the daisied churchyard and the high, fresh-looking village of flint and cream-washed cottages. Saham Toney's Perpendicular beginnings are cruelly overlaid by the precision of an insensitive Gothic Revivalist. Even the ravishing situation of the church, its proximity to an ample Georgian rectory of red brick and its outlook upon a line of willows and alders waving above a wide field of poppies cannot compensate for its want of joy or mystery. Flempton, in a sombre, pine-studded landscape, would make as dismal an impression but for a wall tablet commemorating a rector called Blastus Godly. The massive flint tower is all that remains of the original Ickborough; the glistening nave dates entirely from 1865. Yet, unlike most restored churches, it has both charm and humour. The Victorian sculptor of the colossal gargoyles, spiny-backed monsters and a wry-mouthed man plucking at a stringy beard, has succeeded in giving fresh expression to a medieval idiom. And the whole setting of the church is like a miniature of the fairest aspects of the last century. An old man in a broken panama hat scythes the grass among the tombstones and rakes it into pale green heaps. Below the churchyard wall a wheat field spreads out to the horizon and flows about a comfortable farmhouse with a pretty reed-thatched roof. Opposite the church a row of gabled, one-storyed almshouses exhibits in Gothic lettering the legend: "Abide with us for it is towards evening and the day is spent". A little farther towards the village a war memorial perfectly harmonises with the spirit of the place. It is of white marble and stands in a railed enclosure in a market garden. It represents a lady in the costume of 1890 wearing an embroidered veil and leaning her head against a rock on which hangs a realistic wreath of daisies, ferns and marsh mallows.

A number of Breckland churches resemble private chapels rather than parish churches; they are situated, often some distance from the villages they serve, in the midst of a park, and they are usually kept locked. Culford is hidden away in a great plantation traversed by a moist, violet-scented drive. It is a dark little church, entirely of the last century except for a bust of Sir Nathaniel Bacon and a seated figure of Lady Bacon, builders of the original house. But they are quite overshadowed by the life-sized, white marble effigies of the Cadogans which fill the interior and seem to crowd out any parishioner intrepid enough to share the service with them. At Hengrave, too, the little church is so fully occupied by the relics of the great families who have lived in the Hall that it is impossible to think of it as anything but a private chapel. The seclusion of the building is absolute. Sir Thomas Kytson, his wife Margaret and her third husband, John Bouchier, full-size figures, rest in profound silence broken only when a breeze sets in motion the pines that dwarf the round tower or when the gentle note and the soft splash of a waterbird reverberate from the weed-grown lake beside the church. I have never been able to see the interior of Brettenham, and its cracked, weatherbeaten door looks as though it has not been opened for many years. It is again a tiny, completely restored building but for a Norman arch on the south side, all that survived a fire in 1852. The church stands on the edge of Brettenham Park by the side of a road leading up to the village, but it belongs much more to the Manor than to the village. Round about it flowers a rich water-meadow, cattle browse among the tombstones and a little path netted with bindweed and stonecrop leads from the church, not towards the village but to a lychgate giving directly on to the park. Weeting, very small, round-towered and restored, plays no part in village life and seems no more than a shell now that the Hall lies ruined. Ivy-grown, damp and lost in the ex-tensive park, it is a sad memorial to the departed Angersteins whose epitaphs and monuments adorn its interior.

A tower in a pastoral setting is always a romantic sight. In an austere landscape like that of Breckland the combination of park and church is unusually exciting. When, as occasionally happens, a church has not suffered under the restorer's hand, the beauty of its shape and situation can be overwhelming. I shall never forget the delight with which I first saw Hilborough. I had been bicycling for some hours through plantations and over desolate warrens when suddenly I caught a glimpse of green undulations, streams bright with kingcups, graceful clumps of beech and elm, a distant pale, pedimented façade in the Adam manner, a flock of sheep, and in the centre of it all a church of almost transparent silvery flint with a square tower and a great high clerestory whose wide windows were ablaze in the afternoon light. A fretted parapet, the figure of a saint, carvings of coats of arms and the emblems of St Michael added still greater elegance to the structure while the flintknapper's art was seen at its best in the diapered flushwork of the porch.

West Harling is also most poetically placed. Its likeness to a grey ship floating in a green sea was accentuated, when I last visited it, by a white autumn vapour rising from the ground to about a height of three feet, so that nothing below the nave window-sills was clearly visible, and three little boys playing around a wheelbarrow by the lychgate showed only their heads and shoulders above the mist and looked like swimmers. The merest track led across the grass to the gate, and behind the church the park stretched on uninterruptedly dotted by groups of fir and beech and dominated by an immense, stricken oak between whose bleached boughs hung the fiery November sunball. To the left the park was fringed by a low belt of conifers; a frail sign-post pointed through the trees to Stonehouse Farm, while another, leaning over a sandy path, bore the name Dowerhouse. I found no trace of either.

The interior of the church must always be very dark but it was particularly obscured on that misty afternoon and little could be made out but the hanging oil-lamp and a surprisingly sophisticated eighteenth-century marble bust of a lean, curly-headed man, set in a roundel hollowed from the south wall of the chancel. A slab beneath it bore the following inscription:

Ricardo Gipps
Avunculo suo
Gulielmus Croftes
Hoc Marmor
In grati Animi Testimonium
Poni voluit
Posuit Ricardus Gulielmi Filius.

The proximity of pine forests and the coarseness of the grass mark both Hilborough and West Harling as Breckland's own despite their sylvan beauty. Though they are not so barren of architectural interest as most of the churches so far described, my concern with them has been prompted by their relation to the strange district in which they stand. But there are a few churches in Breckland which demand mention irrespective of their surroundings, and two which are famous beyond the confines of the region: Mildenhall and Swaffham. The tall, graceful tower of Mildenhall, far less massive than most East Anglian towers, can be seen many miles away on the fen side of the town. The view of the tower from the Barton Mills road, a glittering shape, looking, on account of its corner turret, as though it leans against the sky high above roof-tops, willows and flat fields, is like a scene from a medieval book of hours. The impression fades as the town draws nearer. The church is lost to sight and modern villas, forests of television aerials, American accents and uniformed figures from the aerodromes overpower all sense of the past. A cemetery lying in a rough hollow soon, however, awakens new interest. Fluted columns, urns and tombstones of dazzling white marble incline at all angles on the green slopes, entwined with wild roses and viper's bugloss; and on one tomb black Gothic letters spell the entrancing name of Zilpha. Once the town centre is reached something of the peace and security which Mildenhall enjoyed for centuries, first as a Royal Manor of the Abbey at Bury St Edmunds and then as the property of the Norths, the Hanmers and the Bunburys, still survives the glare and fret of neon signs and heavy traffic. A covered Market Cross of the time of

Henry V recalls the great fish market for which this border town was once renowned throughout East Anglia. The Elizabethan Manor House was demolished in 1933, but many ancient timbered houses still exist, including the old Bell Inn and four early Georgian almshouses by the side of the churchyard, built by Sir Thomas Hanmer. They are yet inhabited by four elderly parishioners as the deed of gift originally enjoined.

In the immediate shelter of the magnificent church the incongruous reminders of our own age are all forgotten. The exterior is far more elaborate than that of any other Breckland church. The east end is supported by lacy, canopied buttresses surmounted by octagonal pinnacles, a panelled parapet runs above the north aisle and the wall below is patterned with flint and with freestone. The porch is of unusual size with a vaulted ceiling and bosses covered with emblems of the Evangelists. Over the porch is a small Lady Chapel, now a bare, evenly lit room reached by a stairway at the end of the north aisle. On stepping into the church itself the impression of space and light is so soothing that for a moment every faculty is absorbed in contemplating the colourless panes of the large clerestory windows and the perfect proportions of the slender columned lancet arches. Then the eye is drawn to the remarkable design of the east window, framed by the chancel arch. The window was the work of a gifted vicar, Richard de Wichforde, incumbent of Mildenhall 1309–44. The shallow arch is supported by delicate pillars of Purbeck marble. The cusped lower lights contain scenes of the Passion. Above the central light is a mandorla surrounded by tiny, gleaming quatrefoils. Large quatrefoils, like great jewels, follow the outline of the window and on either side of the mandorla are shapes like large fleurs-de-lis, each enclosing a figure.

Mildenhall is famous for its roof and the light which streams from the windows catches the great pinions of hovering angels, so that for an instant they seem silently to beat the air. These angels clasp shields upon which are carved the instruments and emblems of the Passion, while other lesser angels spread their wings about tie-beam and cornice and display scrolls inscribed with holy messages. This enchanting company of long-robed beings with their compassionate glances, backward blowing curls and long, thin fingers at first demands undivided attention. But gradually the exuberant carvings upon the hammer beams and the huge supporting braces of the aisle roofs come into view. They are the work of an artist whose skill in composition is equalled by his imagination, humour and powerful sense of drama. Fabulous monsters and heraldic devices mingle with vivid scenes from the Scriptures and from legend, the Annunciation, the Baptism, the Adoration of the Shepherds, Abraham and Isaac and St George, a portly, bearded gentleman who plunges his sword into the mouth of a smiling dragon, while the king and queen, two large heads peeping over the top of a castle, watch him with lively interest and the tiny princess kneels in prayer just behind the horse's tail.

Swaffham, too, boasts an angel roof and beautiful angel corbels whose wings frame their heads in a single arc. Among a few carved bench-ends there is only one which is of aesthetic interest. It depicts John Chapman, the Swaffham pedlar, in his shop while his wife looks over the shop door and tells her beads. Nearby is a second carving of the pedlar, with a modern copy close by it, but this would certainly be ignored were it not for its associations. It is a meagre, naturalistic little work showing John Chapman in round cap and belted tunic with his pack on his back and his dog, chained and muzzled, at his side. The story of the pedlar is told with variations in many countries. John Chapman, a pedlar of Swaffham, dreamed that if he went to London Bridge he would hear something to his advantage. He obeyed the dream, travelled to London and for a time wandered about the bridge. At length a man accosted him and asked him what or whom he sought. The pedlar recounted his dream. "If I paid any attention to dreams," said the other, "I should now be in some place called Swaffham, digging under a pear tree in an orchard there, for I've dreamed there's a chest of money lying in that spot. But I don't hold with such things." The sequel is plain: the pedlar made his fortune and built the north aisle of Swaffham Church.

John Chapman's name occurs in the famous Black Book of Swaffham, which is kept in the priest's chamber above the ancient vestry. He is one of a list of creditors to whom the sum of six shillings and eightpence is owed. The book is not black but brown and of insignificant appearance, consisting of but thirty-two leaves of about twelve by four inches bound in a calf cover. Several different handwritings make up a record of various incidents in church and town life from about 1448 to 1460. The church lands are described in detail, there is a long inventory of the church ornaments, vestments and plate and most of the citizens are mentioned by name, either as debtors or creditors or for burning candles before the great crucifix or in "Our Ladies Chapel" on Christmas Day, at the Feast of Epiphany and "the holie Feast of Easter".

The church is memorable, however, not so much for its pedlar, its Black Book or its angel roof, but for its vast, narrow nave and splendid western arch, sweeping up almost to the full height of the lofty interior. Even the over-bright windows of Victorian glass behind it cannot lessen the exhilarating effect of this arch which, in the light streaming from the gooseberry-green glass of the aisle windows, looks like two gigantic rhubarb stems swaying and meeting beneath the sea.

The fine exterior of the church is most rewarding when seen from the luxuriant churchyard, looking towards the east end. The waving pattern of the east window is echoed by the window of the tower, an elegant pinnacled structure with a delicate openwork parapet and a pretty lead spire which was added in the eighteenth century. Swaffham churchyard is one of the pleasantest spots in all Breckland. It is raised above street level like an island, a mysterious place of green, moist shadows and summer scents in the heart of the exposed, wind-beaten, stony little town. Thick, small-leaved ivy clutches tree and tombstone and clings in dense mats about each grassy mound. Yews burst from tangles of briars, ragged lavender bushes obstruct the narrow, weedy paths. Among the gravestones are many striking Victorian examples. One monument to Susan Blythe, tottering beneath its ivy festoons, contains four praying angels in elaborate niches, Pre-Raphaelite creatures with swelling necks, streaming locks and humourless, bugle eyeballs. Others bear strange names in bold jet characters: Gathergood, Loveless, Jeary, Alva and Goodbody. On a hot July evening, magic lies about this churchyard. The bellringers are practising. From the nave all eight of them can be seen at work. They are in their shirt sleeves and one, the leader, is so old and frail that it is a wonder he is not carried up to the top of the tower at the end of the bell rope. They ring every change and at last finish with a mournful single note that lingers among the dark yews and the tombs. Then a fainter and more cheerful sound rests and soars on the evening air. The girls' choir sings next Sunday's psalm.

The delicious scent of lavender mingles with the intoxicating perfume of limes. An avenue of these trees, of great size, ancient and unlopped, leads from the church porch to a lane which gives directly upon the wide market square. The spot is marked by a cross, a domed, Doric-columned edifice with a full, draped figure of Ceres swaying from its summit and clasping a posy. On market days the square is all a-bustle; there is nothing which cannot be bought from the stalls, from cheap jewellery, plates decorated with fantastic versions in strong relief of Flatford Mill and the Haywain to nylon petticoats, fresh flowers and vegetables and poppyseed loaves. And on the broad pavement beneath the church tower, a weekly auction is held of second-hand goods, mahogany tables and chairs with legs like those of high-stepping mares, horsehair sofas, prints of sacred subjects in maple frames, glass pictures and cases of stuffed birds, wax fruits and wool flowers.

The market square is still sometimes the scene of festivals and fêtes, but they can rarely equal in exuberance a festival which was held in 1814 on the afternoon of Thursday, July 7th. An elegantly printed announcement of the proceedings lies on the table before me. The first item on the programme was a donkey race run "by at least four asses, course one heat twice round the Market Place". This was followed by a still more exciting event, a "Shift Race" between four beautiful ladies who, with their high-waisted, diaphanous draperies floating behind them, ran once round the Market Place. The winner, cheerfully applauded, was awarded a finely worked shift with "handsome trimmings", while the second best received a new pair of cotton stockings. Then came another race of asses and ladies together, "but no out of Town asses or out of Town ladies will be permitted to start". The prize was a "set of Tea Equipage" but we do not know whether it was won by an ass or a lady. Chimney-sweep boys next showed their skill of mouth by dipping for shillings in a large bowl of flour with their hands tied behind them. Ladies of all ages competed for a "Ladies Scarlet Spencer, spanking new from London"; the bill adds, however, "No pregnant Lady permitted to run. Decency forbids it." Finally, there was a Royal Pig Hunt round the Market Place. Six strong men ran and the winner carried off the pig. Then, as dusk fell, the west window of the church suddenly shone out through the trees, brilliantly illuminated. It was as if the sun, a single ray of which, slanting through the glass, would wash the masonry of the interior with a gentle flood of light, had withdrawn into the building and was pouring all the fierceness of its concentrated brightness on to the grass and the foliage and the tombs outside. A string band began to play in Church Walk and suddenly hundreds of fireworks went shooting up high above the figure of Ceres. An effigy of Bonaparte, three times as large as life, was carried in procession all round the town, then burnt and blown to pieces on a huge bonfire to the strains of "Go to the devil and shake yourself."

The opposite side of the churchyard looks down upon a country road where a magnificent cedar shades a flint farmhouse neat outhouses and brilliantly coloured implements. Beyond the churchyard, separated from it by a gate and a railing, is a rough common, the most picturesque part of Swaffham. Facing it is a romantic Georgian house with a most unusual, triangular façade. It was once a grammar school and now lies neglected in a wilderness of a garden. Nearby is another group of extraordinarily moving buildings. Of Palladian design and built of mellow red brick, crumbling and weed grown, they look, in their frame of pines, like Hadrian's Villa, and may be part of some ruined or vanished mansion.

Attleborough, on the opposite side of Breckland from Mildenhall, is seldom mentioned in descriptions of East Anglia, though it was once the capital of Norfolk and its church is one of the most astonishing in the country. The little town itself is characteristic of the district and less disturbed by traffic congestion and military manœuvres than Mildenhall, Thetford, Brandon or Swaffham. Red brick and flint houses cluster about a white-railed green, known grandly as Queen's Square, which boasts a café, the Bounty, and an antique shop, two tiny low-ceilinged rooms packed with enticing objects, seventeenth- and eighteenth-century carved stone heads, fragments of columns, Victorian vases of sugar-pink and deepest blue, Staffordshire figures, inlaid boxes, mirrors, prints and needlework pictures. From the Square, Church Street, with a few ancient, half-timbered houses, runs into Thetford Road, where Victorian chapels and villas with Norman doorways, Tudor windows and classical ball ornaments stretch out in a dismal line among flat fields and mouldering allotments. The mixture of styles, the harsh disregard for seemliness force themselves upon the eye more than in other places and emphasise the alien qualities of Breckland.

The church stands on the farther side of the Square raised above street level on high rough ground, a great humped, defiant mass with a Norman half-ruined tower curiously placed at the east end. It was once central but the choir, which extended beyond it, no longer exists. The fortress-like aspect of Attleborough at once commands attention, but the interior makes an even more powerful and lasting impression. Nave and aisles, separated by soaring, very slender columns, form an immense rectangle, almost a square, dramatically, mysteriously lit by exceedingly high, small clerestory windows and by one plain window in the north aisle. Shafts of brightness alternate with impenetrable shadow. The light falls softly upon a wall-painting above the tower arch and concentrates upon a patch of bright colour in the screen immediately below it. Other jewel-like colours flash and disappear into the surrounding dusk. They are seen to be a row of shields bearing the arms of the English sees, running across the whole width of the church and decorating the upper part of an intricately carved and painted canopied rood-screen of the fifteenth century. It is of light oak, so dry that it seems about to disintegrate, yet with a magic quality of growth about it as though it were still part of some ancient, blasted, almost sapless tree, rooted nevertheless and up-raising its leafless limbs to the elements. Six of the panels of this screen are filled with fifteenth-century paintings of St John the Baptist, the Virgin and Child, St John the Evangelist, an Archbishop, the Trinity and St Bartholomew. The detail is obliterated but the figures make a gentle harmony of dull green and rose above floral patterns of gold. A stream of brilliant light pierces the central opening of the screen from a decorated window of modern glass representing the Nativity, the Cruci-fixion and the Ascension. The subjects are tastefully and modestly treated, in no way attempting to vie with the magni-ficent fourteenth-century west window with its clusters of pin-nacles, niches, its leaf-and-flower shapes, angels, shields and crosses. Except for this window the space behind the screen is all Norman work. It contains the altar, but it is more like a chapel than a chancel for, owing to the curious plan of the church, it is cut off from the body of the building.

The perfect proportions, the cathedral-like atmosphere, the wide, honey-coloured floor-stones of this east end of the church must always distinguish Attleborough in recollection, but even more unforgettable are the wall-paintings above the screen. The great arched space is broken by two Norman apertures, one above the other, which were once incorporated in the painted design. But the cross, which occupied part of the upper opening, and the representation of the Annunciation above it have vanished. There remain two tiers of life-sized figures resembling strolling players, though scrolls over their heads bear biblical names. Jeremiah is conspicuous in a tall, round, full hat, a loose green garment cut open at the sides and falling to the knees over a skirt of scarlet and gold; lively angels carry instruments of the Passion, while others, decked with feathers from chin to toe, wear men's fifteenth-century hats and prance along with censers in the shape of Chinese lanterns; an immensely tall thin figure, stretching the whole height of the painting, might well be mounted upon stilts. The mural appears to be executed in oil and, with its exquisite golden yellows, greens and faded reds, delicate drawing and sense of character, must be one of the most accomplished works of the medieval East Anglian school of painting.

Everyone has heard of Castle Acre Priory, but its splendid church is seldom praised. It stands above the Priory at the end of the village, which is one of the most characteristic and exciting places in Breckland. It lies on rising ground overlooking the Nar. Stony fields, patches of heath and gaunt pines make up the typical Breckland scene. A narrow white road leads through the wide, desolate landscape up to Castle Acre, which from a little distance has the appearance of a walled, medieval town, for it is held in the embrace of the gigantic earthworks of the former Castle. Every Castle Acre cottage is of flint, the streets are narrow, steep and pebbly and a great flint, bastioned arch spans the entrance to the main street. Despite the ruin of Castle and Priory the alert, invigorating atmosphere of this village seems successfully to challenge the influence of wind and heath. The battlemented church, long, elegant and silvery, is a testimony of man's triumph over nature. Not a single addition, not a single false note disturbs the calm of the wide, simple interior, which is of Early English design with a graceful east window and a tall western arch. The pulpit, shaped like a wine-glass, dates from 1410 and is adorned with paintings of SS Gregory, Augustus, Jerome and Ambrose, elongated, linear figures with scrolls uncoiling about their heads upon a starry background. The font repeats the shape of the pulpit, but it is surmounted by an astonishing cover, a tower of telescoped Gothic niches, the perch of a gilded dove. The full beauty of the east window, with its roundels and narrow lancets, is best seen from the churchyard. The shining, light grey flints, flecked here and there with yellow and orange, form a perfect setting for the stone mouldings and the simplicity and breadth of the design contrasts with two fussy little Perpendicular windows which break the vestry wall. Upon the panelled parapet sit three great heraldic dogs, casting giant shadows across the grass, where a bony man 'dressed all in black is cleaning a tombstone to one Blogs.

Gooderstone has something of the same atmosphere as Castle Acre. The village looks down upon a stream-laced tract where blue rushes and lettuce-green burdock leave invade the bracken and lichen of the heaths. The cottages, like those at Castle Acre, seem to assert their flintiness. The church, less elegant than Castle Acre, rises up like an immense bulwark against blowing sand and rough weather. I have never heard it commended, but it is one of the most moving buildings I have seen. It is of darkest flint with an imposing, square, almost windowless tower, hoary with weeds and neglect. It is surprising to find within those thick, rude walls a wonderfully preserved and elegant interior, clear and clean as though just washed by the sea. A painted screen divides nave and chancel, a most delicately carved object where naturalistic pinks and thin pointed leaves frame painted panels of saints and angels. The angels all wear crowns and ermine collars and lean forward over a balustrade with looks of astonishment. Though the figures of the saints have been damaged and scratched, enough remains of the original drawing and colouring to show a style closely resembling that of the Attleborough screen. But the interest of the screen is eclipsed by the striking east window of the single aisle.

A cross-eyed God the Father in a robe of seaweed brown dominates the design, scarlet-and-white-gowned angels spread golden wings and fly in all directions and, below, figures clad in white pray in the shade of large, symmetrical yews.

The glass at Gooderstone is like the Winchester illuminations; the better-known glass of East Harling is Flemish in character. It was bequeathed to the church by Sir Robert Wingfield, who died in 1480. In 1641 the glass was removed to preserve it from the iconoclasts and hidden in the attics of East Harling Manor House, the home of the Lovells. There it remained until the Manor was sold in 1736 to Thomas Wright, who restored the window to the church. The entire story of the New Testament is crowded into the lower lights of this great Perpendicular window. The upper lights are taken up with exquisitely drawn, sea-coloured carnations with dark red or green centres and two figures of angels treated in a surprisingly modern decorative manner. One has a transparent body, a watery blue head and nimbus, the other a pale blue body and a white head and nimbus. Among the scenes below, *The Adoration of the Shepherds* is one of the most charming versions of the subject I have seen. The Virgin holds the Child on her lap in front of a manger where a pink ox and ass are feeding. One shepherd kneels and doffs his cap, two others stand behind, one clasping a lamb, the other playing upon a curious pipe. In the foreground is a hen coop in which lie two eggs and on the top of the coop is a large spoon with a pierced handle. *The Betrayal*, with Judas in a brilliant yellow robe, is a most dramatic scene. Malchus, whose ear is about to be cut off by St Peter, wears elaborate, fashionable late fifteenth-century dress. *The Visitation*, another striking panel, also illustrates medieval costume. Elizabeth is wearing a laced robe and a crimson mantle edged with gold, a pleated barbe and a veiled head-dress beneath a black velvet turban. *The Marriage at Cana* demands special attention, for it is an unusual interpretation of the subject. In the foreground sits a woman with a turban upon her head adorned with a flashing jewel. The table is spread with two plates, a fowl and a joint of meat and in front of it stands a strange, nimbed figure holding in one hand a tall, pyramidal cup and in the other a wand. There are six pitchers at his feet, into which a boy pours water. Christ sits to the right of the table with an elderly man and woman on his left. Farther to the right stands Our Lady, who looks imperiously at the nimbed man and points to the pitchers. Who is this man? Is he the master of the feast?

This intriguing window is only one of the treasures of East Harling, the most elegant of all Breckland churches. It makes an impression of exquisite harmony, for the structure dates mainly from the fifteenth century. A high, narrow nave with a hammer-beam roof of pale wood, so steep that it looks like hands touching at the finger-tips in an attitude of prayer, contrasts with spacious aisles flooded with clear light from great Perpendicular windows. The east end of the south aisle is occupied by an elaborate chapel enclosed by a branching screen of fan-vaulted niches and ogee arches adorned with Tudor roses, coats of arms, frilly leaves, small heads, quatrefoils and geometric patterns, all carved with such precision that they have the appearance of being executed in wire. Within this chapel are the tombs of the members of the two great families of East Harling, the Herlings and the Lovells. The effigy of Sir Robert Herling, who died on the battlefield in France in 1435, lies in the corner under an ornate canopy decorated with shield and helmet, horses with lashing tails and a unicorn. Beside him rests his wife, Jane. Figures and canopy are of blanched, polished marble, the extreme pallor of which contrasts with the flamboyant colour of the neighbouring monument to Sir Thomas Lovell and Dame Alice, his wife. Sir Robert Herling's daughter, Ann, had no children and the estate reverted to her aunt, Margaret Tuddenham. Her daughter married Sir Edmund Bedingfield of Oxburgh, who sold East Herling to Sir Thomas Lovell, Chancellor of the Exchequer. It is his descendant and namesake who is buried in the church. He died in 1604 and his tomb is Jacobean in character. The Corinthian capitals of the columns supporting the canopy shine with gold paint; and the structure is richly ornamented with black obelisks, golden balls and complicated strap-work. The knight wears jet black armour and his wife is clad in a black gown. At their feet are their crests, Sir Thomas's a bright bundle of peacock feathers, Dame Alice's a surrealist creation. Two pink arms rise from the tomb and hold aloft what seems to be a human head with a strong brown neck and thick dark curling hair; but it has no features; below the forehead there is nothing but a hollow.

East Harling Church is heated by Victorian stoves, each decorated on top by a tortoise in relief. The church cleaner who tends the stoves is a noticeable figure. He looks as fresh and neat as the interior he cares for so well, with piercing blue eyes and very pink cheeks. He is an old man who has lived all his life in East Harling and he will tell visitors how in his youth he worked on the land for a wage of twelve shillings a week and how it was the custom then for all the poor to flock to the workhouse for the winter, when there was nothing to be done outside.

He is anxious that the porch, completely covered with flush-work, should not be overlooked and insists that the church should be seen from the other side. Beyond the graveyard wall the ground dips down abruptly and the stone-littered fields come into view where the old man toiled as a boy. A break in the ancient, creeper-hung wall gives access to a rough meadow and a decaying circular, red-brick dovecote, topped by a tiny cupola. It is from here that the noble exterior of the church can be best appreciated. The fragile lead spire rises from a cluster of pinnacles set like a diadem above the ornamental parapet of the square tower; the regular rows of tall clerestory and aisle windows sparkle in the afternoon light. It would be difficult to associate so graceful and finished a work of art with Breckland were it not for the character of the adjoining village, the roughness of the meadow grass, the presence of a twisted pine near the dovecote and the ruined aspect of this little building. The classical summit of the dovecote contrasts enchantingly with the Gothic fantasy of the tower, just as its exposed rafters, gaping dormers and the great zigzag rents in its walls emphasise the perfect preservation of the church. It is astonishing that so elaborate a building as East Harling should have risen on the unpromising soil of Breckland and still more surprising that it should have survived. For nearly all attempts to build on a scale exceeding the demands of mere necessity have been overtaken, if not by the restorer's zeal then by ruin. Some of the ruins which are so conspicuously part of the Breckland scene form the subject of the following chapter.

4. BRECKLAND RUINS

The road from Thetford to Rushford passes a hollow in which stands a ruined flint cottage. It is a mysterious place shut in by pine, beech and alder. Ivy grows so thickly about the crumbling flints that it is only by peering closely into the dell that the shape of a house can be made out. Tendrils cling to the chimney-stack and the former positions of doors and windows are marked by five yawning gaps in a curtain of green. Though the ruin is of recent date it is already held to be haunted and no local man willingly travels that way after dark. Lights are said to shine out through the ivy leaves at midnight, white-clad figures appear at the openings wringing their hands, while the hollow resounds with shrieks and groans. There is another supposedly haunted ruin between West Stow and Icklingham. It lies on high ground above a reedy swamp, an abandoned farmstead. The red-tiled roof is rent open and bushes press against the flint walls and choke the entrance. The faded purple door of a pigsty still hangs in position clapping to and fro in the wind and in the yard of the sty and behind the house grow gigantic thorn trees. Anyone who dares to walk under those thorn trees at midnight may hear the wail of a dead girl deserted by her American lover.

Despite shortage of houses, a population unnaturally swollen by an influx of refugees, American airmen and members of Her Majesty's forces from other parts of England, such ruins are common in Breckland. For one reason or another, on account of barren soil, remote situation or perhaps owing to compulsory evacuation by military authorities, it seems a usual fate for the buildings of the district to disintegrate and at last to revert to their beginnings and become piles of loose, rough flints scattered across heath and warren. Decay is, of course, the enemy of all buildings, but nowhere do they seem to succumb with so little struggle as in Breckland. Manifold disasters have befallen Breckland buildings; they have always been doomed. The original great Halls of Ampton and Euston perished by fire; Livermere was demolished a year or two ago; Wretham was devastated by the Army and pulled down; Santon House and Bodney Hall were allowed to disintegrate long before country mansions were threatened by the present economic situation; Wilby Old Hall, a moated seventeenth-century house, was auctioned and ransacked like Hafod in Cardiganshire; Mildenhall Manor was demolished; the Halls of Eriswell and Wangford survive only in part as dilapidated farmhouses. At least six churches, Buckenham Tofts, Caldecot, Colveton, Little Hockham, Lynford and St Martin's, Barnham, have vanished utterly. Roudham was gutted by fire on August 10th, 1736, when a plumber, repairing the lead on the top of the tower, dropped some ashes from his pipe on to the thatched roof. The towers of Great Hockham and of Foulden fell in the early eighteenth century, that of St Nicholas, Feltwell, crashed in 1898; the roof of Little Cressingham collapsed in 1781; lightning struck one of three churches at Beechamwell and another is reduced to craggy fragments. At Oxburgh the landlord of the Bedingfield Arms was looking from his window one day in April 1948 when suddenly he saw the church tower and spire fall and crush the nave.

In a district where zest for restoration often waxed so great, it is extraordinary that these calamities should have been accepted without more attempt to repair the damage. Tradition does indeed record that an appeal for subscriptions to rebuild Roudham met with a most generous response, but that the treasurer decamped with the money, and no further effort was made to save the building. The dread foundations upon which, as Carlyle said, the green of nature everywhere rests seldom reveal their power and hostility so openly as in Breckland, and to those who are sensitive to atmosphere it is significant that most of these accidents to churches have taken place either in the eighteenth century, when feeling for established religion was at its lowest ebb, or in our own time, when it is often economically impossible to effect a rescue.

There were various monastic establishments in Breckland, at Eriswell, Cockley Cley, Hilborough, Weeting, Thetford and Castle Acre, but with the exception of the two last nothing but a few broken flints and fragments of masonry bear witness to their existence. At Thompson the remains of a college for secular canons, founded in the reign of Edward I and enlarged in 1349 by Sir John de Shardelow, have been incorporated in a farmhouse. All that can be traced of the former college are two double-arched Tudor windows, a doorway with a four-centred arch, remnants of a cell and the sites of two old fish-ponds. The former chapel of St Lawrence at Eriswell, a mixture of flint, brick, half-timber and wattle and daub, has been used in the past as a granary and stands, now cracked and neglected, in the middle of a turnip field.

Norman castles are rarely other than ruinous, but those erected in Breckland, Old Buckenham, built by a follower of William the Conqueror called William d'Albini, Weeting and Castle Acre, both the work of William de Warrenne, have reached the final stage of dissolution and will soon be remembered only by mighty rampart or weed-encumbered moat.

Decay accords well with Breckland; and I recall the moments when I have been confronted for the first time with some stricken Breckland church or mansion as among the more memorable in my experience. No artificial ruin, no relic of former magnificence carefully preserved by the State could be as moving as the fissured tower, the falling arches and the roof-less, overgrown nave of solitary Roudham. Roudham is altogether a place of enchantment, a heathland village of scattered cottages without even an inn. The winding road which connects the houses is known as "The Street" and two sandy lanes which lead into this road from Roudham Heath are called "Street Gate" and "Ringle Gate". After crossing the exposed heath these tracks, fringed by tall grasses and thorn trees, make an impression of delicious verdour and intimacy. Then suddenly, above a group of tiny red-brick cottages framed by lime and elm, a decaying flint tower adorned with a monstrous fish-eyed gargoyle appears against the sky. The next moment the lane enters The Street and the full impact of the ruined church is felt. Enough of the tower survives to show that it must once have been extremely graceful. There are remains of a pretty parapet, and the entrance to the church, which was under the tower, is surmounted by a charming cusped niche and a circular opening. A great bush half covers the doorway and the threshold is deep in nettles which seem to have thrived undisturbed for many years. They have taken complete possession of the west end of the nave. Grasses, poppies and dog daisies ripple up to the chancel where the superb arch of the east window, which alone stands entire, spans the space between the decomposing, ivy-matted walls. Elder bushes flank the nave, and at the season when they flower their white disks shine out against the dark undergrowth and the ruined walls as bright lamps must once have glowed in the dusk of the church. To the west, beyond the tower, a rude triangle of flint, pierced by a narrow, creeper-curtained opening, and an iron railing mark the enclosure where rest members of the Boyce family. Their tombs and monuments are almost concealed by the vigorous growth of the nettles.

A family of jackdaws has its nest in the tower. One day when I was visiting Roudham a young bird, nearly fully fledged but still helpless, had fallen to the ground. He moved clumsily but rapidly away at the sound of my approach and, terror-stricken, found a perch among the mouldering stones of the Boyce chapel. In his brilliant eye, regarding me fixedly through the nettles, was concentrated all the disquiet which I felt everywhere within the walls of the ruin. I could not stay there a moment longer. A storm was coming up as I mounted my bicycle and turned towards Bridgeham. By the gates of Roudham Hall, a Georgian house in a large, untended park, I glanced back at the doomed church. It was a dramatic sight. The vast pale arc of the chancel window and the jagged tower immediately behind it, colossal in scale beside the cottages and flat fields, flashed against the ominous sky and reminded me of the tempest scene in Green's toy theatre sets for *Dick Whittington*.

The ruins of Foulden and Oxburgh are as evocative as those of Roudham and as characteristic of Breckland. Foulden is a larger village than Roudham, and lies about the margins of a marshy common. It is two hundred years since the church tower fell, but the rubble piles against the west end as though the disaster occurred less than a week ago. Shorn of the tower, this west end makes a fine composition above the mass of broken masonry and flints. The disorder of the debris is emphasised by the regular shapes of the cherub-headed tombstones in the square churchyard and by the neatness of a flint cottage to the right of the nave.

Oxburgh is a gaunt, deserted place with a dark, yellow brick inn, a few bleak cottages and a clump of pines. Its ruin is the most extraordinary of any I have seen. Only the chancel is still intact. All the rest of the church, except for a small clearing in the south aisle, is one vast heap of loose flints, shattered stonework and plaster crushed to powder. Ferns, rosebay, elder and ash have already taken root and flourish upon the wreckage. Tossed high on the ruinous mass, an immense bell lies where it fell on the day of the disaster with its rusty clapper beside it. Broken oil-lamps, parts of carved bench-ends, the stone head of a man pulling his left ear, another headless carving of a furry creature with big, webbed feet, sodden, bursting hassocks, a piece of faded red carpet with black fleur-de-lis on it—all these can be distinguished among the fragments of masonry.

It is possible with some effort to clamber over the confusion of ruin and to stand in what was once the south aisle, now open to the sky and beset with weeds. At the end of this aisle, separated from it by a grille, is one of the most striking monuments in Breckland, the Bedingfield chantry, which has fortunately escaped destruction. It was built for Margaret Bedingfield after her death in 1514 and houses several tombs, one of which, nameless and dateless, at once catches the eye. Seen through the foliage of two thick elder bushes it might be some exotic Mexican work of art. Of palest terracotta, a medium brought to this country by Italian workmen and seen again at Great Cressingham Manor, it is a fantastic assemblage of round-arched niches, obelisks, swelling bastions and pilasters with intricate, composite capitals. Every inch of the surface is covered with ornament, plant forms, urns, cherub heads and geometric configurations, a curious instance of Renaissance motives imposed on purely Gothic feeling. Other monuments in the chantry include a baroque design with a bat-winged death's head wreathed with laurel and bescrolled Queen Anne carving with weeping cherubs, and a grey marble urn festooned with realistically rendered roses, plums, pears, phlox and lilies.

Weeting, near Brandon, affords a less dramatic but nevertheless unforgettable spectacle of ruin. The great park lies like an oasis in the heart of brecks, heaths and fir plantations, romantic and indescribably melancholy in its present state of neglect. Beautiful groups of chestnuts and beech trees yield vistas more ravishing than they could ever have been when the trees were better tended and of more manageable size. On the edge of the park is a row of pretty thatched cottages from which a path leads straight to the Hall. This is a vast neo-classic mansion of red brick which replaced an earlier house and is now itself fast decaying. The wide, pillared porches back and front are split, purple glass has fallen from the lower windows and lies scattered on the green, weed-covered steps at the rear of the house and on the almost obliterated paths and terraces. Immediately next to the house, Polish refugees and forest workers occupy a collection of wooden huts and breed ducks and cattle. It is strange to think that this was once the home of the Angersteins and that here hung the masterpieces belonging to John Julius Angerstein which formed the nucleus of the National Gallery collection. Among them were Claude's *Cephalus and Procris* and *The Embarkation of the Queen of Sheba*, Correggio's *Mercury Instructing Cupid before Venus,* Titian's *Venus and Adonis* and Piombo's *Raising of Lazarus.* The dark, penetrating eyes and decisive features of Angerstein himself are known to us from his portrait by Lawrence, also in the National Gallery.

Near the little church of All Saints, already described, and approached through a gate in the churchyard, is a spot where ruin assumes a more familiar guise. Instead of the plant-grown neglect which precedes disintegration or the chaos of a sudden collapse, a few tidily-kept piles of flint stand on a strip of vivid shaven grass. They are the remains, preserved by the State, of Weeting Castle. Yew trees thrust closely and wildly about a square moat which encloses the Castle and is so covered with pondweed that it looks like a smooth path. It is a poetic place, especially in summer when butterflies from the nearby warrens, the bright orange Small Heath, the Common Blue and the Small Copper fly against the sombre trees and settle on the flints, spotting them with glowing colour.

The River Nar flows by two of the finest ruins in Breckland or indeed in Norfolk, Pentney Gatehouse and Castle Acre Priory. The tiny village of Pentney marks the meeting-place of Breckland and the Fens, and here river and landscape undergo a noticeable change. As it runs out into the marshlands the stream suddenly seems to fill its banks to overflowing; neither trees nor rushes shade its course; it stretches without mystery between fields that are wide and flat, tamed and tilled; the Breckland Nar is wild and secret, it meanders through little verdant valleys where gentle slopes obscure the distant view, willows incline over the water casting a gloom of dark green on beer-bottle brown and the banks are root-knotted, riddled with cavernous recesses and shielded by thick fringes of sedge and willowherb. On either side, beyond the ribbon of green, rough, tawny meadows and stony brecks of great extent show paler than the midsummer sky. In one of these unkempt fields above the river, beside a rutted lane, stands a broken medieval cross. A headless shaft upon a massive, buttressed flint base soars up over the landscape. It is like a lighthouse on a rock; time and weather, like consuming waves, have nibbled and worn away the foot of the plinth; and just as seaweed and limpets clutch the rock, so long-tendrilled ivy and flat, striped snails hold fast to the cross and slowly devour it.

This is a strange enough sight in such a spot, yet it is but a prelude to a more impressive ruin, the gatehouse of a vanished abbey, set quite close to the cross, all solitary in a field at the end of a long winding lane. Though marked on the Ordnance Survey map, it is not easy to find; villagers direct inquirers to the cottage by the level-crossing gates, which is known to them as the "gatehouse", and it is only by a happy chance, guided by the shaft of the cross, that the traveller suddenly finds himself face to face with the noble, desolate relic. It surmounts a slight eminence and is all that survives of a fifteenth-century house of Augustinian canons, a turreted, crenellated structure of flint and freestone with wide arches and traceried windows. It is still possible to climb the stone corkscrew staircases inside the turrets, to stand by the paneless windows, touch the cold sill, pluck the weeds rooted in the time-loosened masonry and to listen to the sound, colossally magnified in the well-like quiet of that forsaken place, of small falling flints set in motion by the intruder.

The charm of this romantic, neglected ruin is eclipsed by that of the far better known and well-cared for remains of Castle Acre Priory. It lies spread upon immaculate lawns below the church and is approached by way of a lane and a well-preserved fifteenth-century gatehouse of flint and brick. To the right of the gatehouse is a large farm beside a field flushed with

4* 49

the scarlet of poppies. A massive barn looks as though it were once part of the monastic buildings. The path curves a little from the gatehouse and sweeps up to the west front of the former Priory church. It is a composition of breath-taking beauty. Three tiers of wall arcades, the upper and lower interlacing, fill the bottom half, while the top is pierced by a large Perpendicular window. The round-headed entrance is framed with mouldings of extraordinary delicacy and variety, chevrons and ropes, detailed geometric lacy patterns of Moorish flavour, and one design resembling dried figs on a string. The rows of arcading are separated by bands of carved stonework like elongated strips of fragile, finely decorated pastry. Above the arcading stretches a row of highly formalised animal and human heads, among them a magnificent bull; and between the arches of the central arcade are small suns intensifying the pagan character of the façade. Two massive square towers once flanked the façade. Of one, little more survives than the wall which forms part of the main front; the other is truncated and broken, yet still stands four storeys high, its delightful ornament of arcading untouched by decay. Making a right angle with this north tower are the Prior's Lodging and the Priory Porch. These two buildings show little signs of ruin. They were altered during the seventeenth century, long after the dissolution of the Priory, and their juxtaposition to the church façade accentuates the homely character of mullioned window and low gable. The wide entrance arch of the porch is surmounted by a very broad band of flint and stone chequer work; the rest of the buildings are all of rough flints. Some of the rooms inside the Lodging are intact and they are of pleasing domestic proportions. The square, shallow chambers on the first floor, which were once the Prior's solar and chapel, retain most noticeably the character of friendly, inhabited apartments, though they are bare of furniture. Richly carved and painted fireplaces are conspicuous features of both rooms and both are steeped in light, one from a great round-fronted oriel, the other from a square Tudor window. There is no trace of ecclesiastical atmosphere about the chapel with its beamed and moulded ceiling painted with faded red and white roses, but in the solar a tiny lavatory basin with a trefoliated head above it recalls the original purpose of the room. A whole colony of swifts nests under the eaves of the Prior's Lodging and they may be seen from the oriel window wheeling and circling over the grass which is nowhere so soft and of such enamelled brilliance as in the angle made by the solar and chapel wall and the Priory church.

Though the official guide to the Priory enables the visitor to reconstruct in imagination the original appearance of the great church and the claustral buildings, to the actual eye very little exists behind the grand façade and the Prior's Lodging. There is nothing but two isolated, rugged flint piers supported and joined by a modern arch, poor stumps of pillars sunken into the turf, fragments of immensely thick walls bearing traces of former decoration and pierced by cavernous recesses and great heaps of grass-grown flints that look like limpet-encrusted rocks. Two rude, shaggy columns frame a view across breck and cornfield of the Perpendicular tower of Castle Acre church.

William de Warrenne, 1st Earl of Surrey, is generally named as the founder of the Priory, but it is now established that the monastery owed its existence to his son William, the 2nd Earl. It was a cell of the Cluniac Priory of St Pancras at Lewes and building operations may have begun in 1090. The character of the architecture of the earliest remains precludes a date later than about 1100. The history of the monastic community is obscure, but the few glimpses afforded by contemporary records of events connected with the Priory suggest that despite many benefactors, great possessions, an ample revenue and an annual sum derived from the exhibition of a valuable relic, the arm of St Philip, the establishment never flourished. In 1259 the Prior of Castle Acre was punished because he had pledged the seal of the convent on behalf of secular persons; in 1283 Prior William fortified the monastery against the Prior of Lewes; in 1293 the Priory was in debt to the extent of "a thousand marks sterling"; in 1294 it was reported that the number of monks at Castle Acre was excessively diminished; in 1351 the king instructed his serjeant-at-arms to arrest the monks of Castle Acre who had "spurned the habit of their order and were vagabonds in England in secular habit". These and other scandals make up what is known of the domestic history of Castle Acre. When it was surrendered to Henry VIII in 1537 there were only ten monks in residence, although the full complement should have been thirty or even more. The property was granted to Thomas Howard, Duke of Norfolk, then passed during the reign of Elizabeth to Thomas Gresham, who conveyed it to Thomas Cecil. His son sold it to Sir Edward Coke, from whose descendant, the Earl of Leicester, it came into the care of the Ministry of Works. Although raised with such enthusiasm and constructed so stoutly, the Priory began to decline almost at once. It shares the fate of many another monastery on English soil, but it seems unlikely that any such venture could have hoped for success in Breckland. As in the gloomy valley of the Honddu, where ill-fated Llanthony was set, there was something in the atmosphere of the site that foretold disaster.

William de Warrenne's castle has reached an even further stage of disintegration than the Priory; it is indeed scarcely to be distinguished from field and heath. The place is marked by a few remnants of thick, hoary walls and by vast ramparts threaded by chalky paths. They clasp the northern end of the village like giant arms and command superb views over red-tiled roofs, tilled fields, warren and marsh. These ramparts, and the walls as well, are beset with bushes and covered with fine turf, harebells and scabious, upon whose purple flowers shiny, red soldier flies gather in hundreds. It is an exhilarating spot, never without a breeze on the most sullen day and with none of the melancholy conventionally associated with ruin. The finest work of architecture could not harmonise more perfectly with the wild spirit of Breckland than these mouldering flints and grassy earthworks. Scarcely any attempt to build nobly in

Breckland has succeeded; it is contrary to the essential character of the place. Only prehistoric man, it seems, was entirely at one with heath and warren; and he alone was able to set upon it his permanent seal. Traces of his work will still be found in the sand when not one stone remains upon another of monastery, church and mansion.

5. COTTAGES OF FLINT

From the parlour window of the Albert Victor at Castle Acre the visitor looks out on a scene which is becoming ever more rare in England, a village in which no foreign element disturbs the strong sense of locality. The individuality of each of the regions which make up the richly varied tapestry of our landscape is most clearly, most movingly expressed in those humble buildings, cottage, barn, farmhouse and inn, which are composed of the earth or the stone upon which they stand. The row of little houses opposite the Albert Victor, the massive medieval gateway and the cottages lining the narrow street running down from it are all of flint, formal projections of the stony soil on which they stand. Building traditions have suffered as harshly in Breckland as elsewhere; alien, standardised materials have replaced native flint and the cottages and council houses erected today are indistinguishable from those which are destroying regional characteristics in every county. New Town, Thetford, is built of the same pallid machine-made bricks and follows the same standard design as groups of council houses in such widely different settings as Broxbourne, Hertfordshire, or Crewkerne, Somerset. The unsightly buildings on the outskirts of Mildenhall have their exact counterparts in most of the southern and midland counties. But the forbidding aspect of Breckland has not encouraged such extensive building as that which has devastated more congenial territories; in the more isolated villages the population has declined rather than increased and often, as at Castle Acre, the domestic architecture continues unimpaired to express the essential character of Breckland.

Castle Acre lies on the edge of Breckland and the cottages here are constructed of the rounded cobbles so frequently seen in north Norfolk, or of cobbles mixed with knapped flints. In the districts supplied by the Brandon knappers dressed flints were principally used for churches and important secular buildings, while rough flints were considered good enough for cottages. But in the centre of Breckland, in the vicinity of Brandon, seventeenth- and eighteenth-century cottages were often built entirely of knapped flints and the nineteenth century is represented by whole terraces of shining black, neatly jointed flints. At Eriswell the small octagonal panes of Gothic Revival windows, outlined in white, charmingly echo the shapes of the dark glassy flints of the walls. A modest farmhouse near Ickborough, a simple box-shaped house with a central porch supported on slender iron columns, is composed of halved flints so beautifully shaped that the first impression is that the walls are made of squares of black crystal. At Icklingham and Lackford, at Lakenheath, Brandon and Thetford, the sun glitters on façade after façade of dressed flint, on row upon row of severe, little flint rectangles of houses. Many of these cottages were originally thatched; the old form of roofing is still occasionally to be seen, as in isolated examples at Hilborough, Wangford and Brettenham, but they are mostly covered now with pantiles or slates which do nothing to soften the austerity of the flint. Such flint cottages, however, have an air of solidity and durability which is denied to cosier-looking dwellings of wattle and daub, clunch or cob.

The popular conception of the country cottage, thatched, half-timbered and rose-embowered, is belied in every Breckland village. The view from the corner of the Wangford road in Lakenheath is typical and it is as grim as many a townscape in the East End of London. The immensely long village street stretches away to right and left as far as the skyline, scarcely rising above it so closely do the houses hug the ground. A few stone-loving plants such as the house-leek cluster at the foot of a wall here and there, but for the most part not a blade of grass softens the harsh angle of ground and façade, not a leaf breaks the straight lines of terraced roofs against the sky; and the walls themselves are broken but by small, widely spaced windows. Were it not for the sparkle of East Anglian light on the flint surfaces, were it not for the dustless paint on doors and window frames, it would be hard to believe that this street led not to factory and warehouse but to wild heaths and forests. At Icklingham again a terrace of bleak cottages of knapped flints, dated 1830, rises sheer from the pebbly road, their starkness emphasised by a few pines straggling along beside the road where the buildings come to an end. The conjunction of such fantastic trees with such black walls could occur nowhere but in Breckland. The flints here are exceptionally dark and exceptionally well-dressed, the joints being so fine as to be almost invisible; the pines are strikingly contorted. One twisted monster has thrust out a branch so savagely towards its neighbour that it has grown fast to the writhing trunk; the knotted roots rearing from the earth are also intertwined and, though their wild attitudes have all the semblance of movement and freedom, these two must remain forever locked together.

Though flint was used in Breckland at the beginning of the Middle Ages for churches, religious houses, castles and manors, the humbler buildings of the period were, as elsewhere in England, of such frailty that none have survived; they consisted but of daubed stakes or of the least durable timber. These cots were replaced by half-timbered cottages during the Elizabethan era and it was only after shortage of wood became extreme in Breckland at the beginning of the seventeenth century that flint came into general use for the building of cottages and farmhouses. Whenever a flint cottage or farmhouse of earlier date than the seventeenth century is found, it is certain that it was originally the dwelling of neither a labourer nor a yeoman tenant of the period but that it has descended in the social scale. There is a most interesting example of such a house at Castle

Acre, old Mr Chater's cottage, known as Dyke Hill, which was perhaps once connected with the Priory or the Castle or served as a steward's house. It stands at the end of the village on high ground above the Nar, within a stone's throw of the ramparts of William de Warrenne's castle. It is a Tudor structure, a simple rectangle buttressed at the eastern end and surmounted there by an enchanting finial of moulded brickwork. The steep roof, once thatched, is now covered with pantiles and the original arched doorway has been filled in with rubble. One of the long sides of the house faces the road and is without a single opening, a sheer cliff-like wall of small, glittering, neatly dressed flints. From this side no one would guess that the austere building could be other than a huge barn, granary or warehouse. A gate at the side leads into the roughest and stoniest of meadows and to Mr Chater's door, a glass-paned door adjoining the Tudor opening. Four square-headed, latticed windows enliven the surface of this wall and all the paraphernalia of cottage life is heaped against the flint. Strings of onions and dried herbs hang on the wall, a huge rainwater butt stands by the door, a dog-kennel, a ginger and white enamel bath, a broken chair, old sacks, a pail of potatoes and a pile of plant pots litter the narrow path and the minute strip of garden separating the cottage from the meadow. A dog and two cats sun themselves amid the disorder and two black cocks quarrel over five hens.

The noble interior has been made to conform as far as possible with the cottager's conception of homeliness. A large, lofty room, which takes up the whole of the lower floor and was probably the great hall of the house when it was first built, has been divided into two. The principal part, still as grandly proportioned as a ducal chamber, has become the cottage parlour. A brown-and-cream wallpaper with a narrow brown frieze covers the walls, a grey carpet with pink roses on it takes up half the floor, and about the circular dining-table, across which runs a strip of white linen, embroidered and lace-edged, stand arm-chairs and a sofa upholstered in a large leafy pattern of bright and dark blue. A screen with a strap-work design embroidered on it in coloured wools half conceals the modern red-brick fireplace; and round the room hang family photographs and oleographs of a winter landscape with children and a snow-man and of a dark interior with a doctor and a sick child. An oil-lamp and an aspidistra stand in the window. But all these objects are rendered pathetic, insignificant and embarrassed by the exquisitely carved beams of the stately Tudor ceiling. A former tenant whitewashed these beams in a vain attempt to cloak their unhomely magnificence and the whitewash still clings to every crevice of the wood. A door by the fireplace leads into the kitchen, a long, narrow, high room to which, however, a cast-iron kitchen range, handsomely adorned with robust flowers and fruits, lends a cheerful note. Mr Chater's sister-in-law, who is at the same time his housekeeper, does all her cooking on this range; and though she has bought an electric reading-lamp with a parchment shade ready for the day when electricity comes to Castle Acre, the oil-lamp remains the only source of evening light at Dyke Hill.

Such architectural splendours as those of Dyke Hill are rarely found in the humble dwellings of Breckland. The interiors of the austere flint cottages reveal little of structural interest apart from the varied examples of the cast-iron worker's art shown in kitchen grates and ranges. Some of them are Victorian, with a boiler on one side of an ornate grate and an oven at the other, while in many instances iron pots and saucepans stand on an Edwardian range, the oven front of which gleams with polished steel. In nearly every case the ornament merits attention; sometimes the design may consist merely of mouldings based on the well-worn acanthus and egg and dart motives, but in other cases large rosettes, bunches of grapes, ivy leaves, stars and, in a cottage at Bodney, lions' heads burst from oven and boiler doors. It is surprising how these relics of half a century and more ago linger on in the isolated villages of Breckland, surprising how many cottagers live in conditions which are now only part of country life in the most remote and inaccessible districts. Though television aerials start up from cottage roofs in the unlikeliest places, they are no more than reminders of the sets that may materialise when modern amenities are available. Water must still be fetched from the pump in all but those villages which happen to lie on main roads, and often after dark there is no illumination in the village street but the soft yellow beams from lamps in cottage windows.

Breckland cottagers are not yet aware of the vogue for re-productions of Van Gogh's pictures which has long since swept the humbler homes of England; in retaining the sepia prints of highland cattle browsing by misty lakes, the large, coloured versions of "Bubbles" and "Orphans", the souvenir china and the gay biscuit-tins which their parents and grandparents treasured, they unconsciously follow the most sophisticated taste of today. Many a fashionable Londoner might feel the urge of the acquisitive instinct if he could see the pictures and knick-knacks of a Breckland parlour. But, to the owners, these objects are neither fashionable nor old-fashioned, they are merely expressive of a way of life which is still largely deter-mined by tradition, as much part of it as the smell of baking bread in the kitchen or the live coals in the smoothing iron.

The conventional idea of a cottage embraces also the cottage garden. But many of the Breckland cottages already described have no gardens. At Lackford a pair of cottages with the pretty pointed windows of the Gothic Revival stand in miserable yards where nothing grows but one or two scraggy cabbages. This is typical of Breckland; untidy, stone-strewn, neglected patches are part of the village scene. In other parts of England the cottager is noted for the care and hard work he lavishes on his garden: nothing, neither an arduous calling nor the fact that he rents and does not own his house and garden, can quench his personal joy in it. Each man has his own special ways of managing a garden, following precepts which seem to be based on a delightful mixture of sense and superstition. "Plant a small fig-tree in an old boot," said an Essex man; "and plant a big one in an old leather trunk. Fig-trees thrive on decomposing

leather—there's nothing better." His further advice was:
"Never sow or plant in a waning moon." The cottage plot of
more fertile regions, well stocked with fruit trees, with luscious
currants, raspberries and strawberries, and gay with flowers, is a
rare phenomenon in Breckland, and yet the inhabitants are as
English as their neighbours and whenever nature relents they
will try to make a garden. At Hilborough walls of big, halved
flints glinting like black metal make a splendid foil to long,
narrow flower strips. Crimson and white and purple phlox,
cabbage roses, marguerites, snapdragons and Canterbury bells
make a far greater impression of colour and abundance than if
they were growing in some district where such sights were
frequent. I still think of the scent of those phlox and of a low
bush completely starred with plump, pink, closely wrapped
roses. Above the flowers a thin pale face showed at one of the
bedroom windows. An old man confined indoors with some
long illness was watching his garden as anxiously as if the soil
were the best in England and his livelihood depended on it. He
could see his neighbours making the most of the summer evenings while the disorder of his own little garden was daily growing greater, and half his failure to get well again was just
because he was not out there at work like the man next door.

Later, at the White Swan, I overheard two men talking about
their gardens. They were discussing the advantages of blackthorn ash for onion beds and went on to remind one another
that potatoes which had been set before Good Friday could not,
of course, be expected to prosper. Though nature so often re-
duces them to despair, the instinct of Brecklanders for digging
and hoeing is not a jot weaker than that of country people
everywhere in England.

As many as twenty-seven of the lonely villages of Breckland
are without even an inn and the inhabitants must seek refresh-
ment and company in other parishes. This is but one more
manifestation of the poverty of the soil and the sparseness of
the population. Yet there is little sign that the people are dis-
contented with their lot. They are indeed to be envied by those

to whom so unsophisticated a mode of life is no longer possible. And surely no one could pass his childhood more happily than in one of these isolated spots. The passage of twenty years has made no difference to the pleasures of the young in the heathland villages; I find the children embarking on their long summer holidays on the same adventures which once made my own blood run fast. All day they roam about the heath entirely caught up in the magic of the open air, freedom and imagination. The keeper is their sworn enemy and it is the exciting awareness of his ever-lurking presence that spurs them on to snare rabbits and look for young pheasants. There is nothing more fearful or more exhilarating than the chase that follows detection, no more side-splitting laughter than that which bursts forth when the keeper is hampered by his bicycle and must struggle over rough ground without a hope of overtaking the miscreants, wheeling the precious vehicle from which nothing will part him.

CHAPTER III

SAND

I. HEATH AND WARREN

IF the flinty character of Breckland asserts itself the moment the traveller sets foot in the district, another element, as fundamental as the first, is soon encountered. When the main roads are abandoned the tracks through plantations and across heaths are seen to be all of sand, sometimes as loose and fine as the sand of the seashore. The landscape in all directions is scarred by sandpits whose sides are riddled with holes, the nests of sandmartins and wheatears. It was thought at one time that this sandy soil was swept by floods into Breckland from the dunes on the banks of the Wash, but it seems that the area was originally covered with a peculiarly sandy type of chalky boulder clay. The chalk was gradually dissolved by the rains and the sand was redistributed by the winds. There is still much movement of sand in wild weather, especially in spring, creating in the heart of fertile England miniature replicas of the wastes of the Sahara. In former days, when the whole countryside was open, this process was not only more frequent but much more violent. During the seventeenth century the village of Santon Downham was almost buried in a sandstorm which raged for over a week, and the Little Ouse was blocked. John Evelyn, visiting Euston in 1677, wrote of "The travelling sands, about ten miles wide of Euston, that have so damaged the country, rouling from place to place and like the Sands in the Desert of Lybia, quite overwhelmed some gentlemen's whole estates." Less than twenty years ago a farmer in this district described his

61

land thus: "Times thass in Norfolk, bor, times thass in Suffolk. That dew dipind which way the wind's a blowin'."

The most interesting consequence of this sandy soil of Breckland, as I have already mentioned, is that, where it has been left undisturbed, not only does that wild life flourish which is common to all heaths, but birds, plants and insects are found which are usually restricted to the coast. Unfortunately, despite its unique value not only to naturalists but to all who respond to the call of the wilderness, the expanse of open heathland is diminishing with every year. This is due not only to the work of the Forestry Commission, which will be described later, but to the activities of the military authorities. A great stretch of heath between Croxton and Wretham is inaccessible, there are camps on Thetford Heath, on the warrens at Livermere and Ingham, near Brandon, Lakenheath and Mildenhall, and Berner's Heath is used as an Air Ministry bombing ground. Sometimes, as between Mildenhall and Shippea Hill, the landscape is disfigured not only by wooden huts and concrete runways but by hideous salmon-pink brick buildings of two or more storeys. Often when I have returned to some favourite heath, Roudham or Wretham or Wangford Warren, I have been held up by a red flag and a notice inscribed: "It is dangerous to cross the heath when the red flag is flying", and once I was prevented from getting down to the water at Langmere by a large white board informing me that the area was full of unexploded bombs. On the days when the red flag is out, and there are many of them, the essential quality of the heath, its solitude, is utterly destroyed. Aeroplanes roar overhead, guns explode every three minutes, officers bellow commands, and tanks rattle at frightening speed one behind the other over the heaths, leaving in their wake barren, impassable tracks of powdery, deeply churned sand.

When at last this frenzied activity ceases and silence descends once more on the warren, it is not the unravished silence of centuries. The sense of spacious repose, impressing upon man his own insignificance, has departed from the landscape as surely as it has gone from Hampstead Heath. Yet future years may perhaps know it again, for the life of the wilderness endures and, strangely, does not appear to have suffered great harm from this rude intrusion.

Mr Drewery, the Brandon flintknapper, told me a year or two ago that I should find stone-curlews nesting where Roudham joins Bridgeham Heath and, though the red flag was out and tanks were in motion, I decided to make an attempt to reach the spot he had described. It was early June but extremely chilly and grey. Spring comes late to Breckland and the heath was covered with young, tender bracken fronds so that it looked in parts like a swelling lawn and reminded me of Keats's description:

> Of unmatured green valleys cold,
> Of the green, thorny, bloomless hedge,
> Of rivers green with spring-tide sedge,
> Of primroses by shelter'd rills
> And daisies on the aguish hills.

The heath sloped upwards and I kept close to a ragged hedge as far away as possible from the mock battle which was raging to my right. The hedge at last joined a track running at an angle to it and following a row of pines. The man-made clamour slowly receded into the background and after a time, when I thought I had come to the place indicated by Mr Drewery, I sat down. The only bird I saw was a pheasant, which made off with a raucous cry as I took up my position. But overhead, persisting through the bark of guns, the thrilling, continuous song of larks informed the subdued day with an air of expectancy. Wild pansies of unusually large size were growing at my feet and under the pines a network of thyme, beginning to break into flower, made a shadow of delicate heliotrope, which, when I looked more closely at it, was mingled with the brown of sandsedge, a flower of the coast. In the green of a shallow, bone-dry ditch behind the trees hundreds of orange and black striped caterpillars were looping themselves about stem and leaf.

Then there was a flash of white against the pines. It was a stone-curlew. The bird alighted a few yards from where I was sitting, then ran along the ground with shapely raised wings. Its plumage, which underneath had looked so pale in flight, now showed itself to be the colour of sand and flint. The wings were folded and for a moment the creature was perfectly still, hardly differentiated from its surroundings. It must have sensed my alien presence, as these shy birds always do, although I was absolutely motionless, for I had scarcely observed its large size, the powerful beak, shorter and straighter than the great curved beak of the curlew of the north, scarcely had time to mark its yellow, expressionless eye, when with conspicuous movements of its highly developed shanks and with its bullet head lowered, it ran rapidly away and was lost almost instantly to view. I made as cautiously as possible towards the spot where it had vanished, but there was no sign of the bird.

During that brief encounter the stone-curlew had remained mute. But there was a shower soon afterwards and when it had passed I was excited and gratified to hear the shrill, repeated call of a number of these birds, a wild, jubilant, yet eerie cry in that grey weather. It resembled the note of the common curlew, but was higher pitched and more drawn out. Then came an answering faint, sobbing "Willie R–e–e–ve" from some far-away heath towards the Little Ouse. It was like the voice of the warren itself, something immutable that could not be killed or enslaved by man's ephemeral doings.

W. G. Clarke, who knew every haunt of the stone-curlew, reported that, like other immigrants, the bird returned each year to within a few yards of the same spot to nest. It would apparently take more than military manœuvres to dislodge such creatures of habit. One bird even went so far as to overcome the traditions of its race and to lay its eggs in thick cover instead of in the open when it discovered that its native heath had become a conifer plantation. But in general planting,

Gooderstone Warren

Twisted pine trees near Oxburgh

Peddar's Way

Aaron's rod growing on the edge of Snake Wood

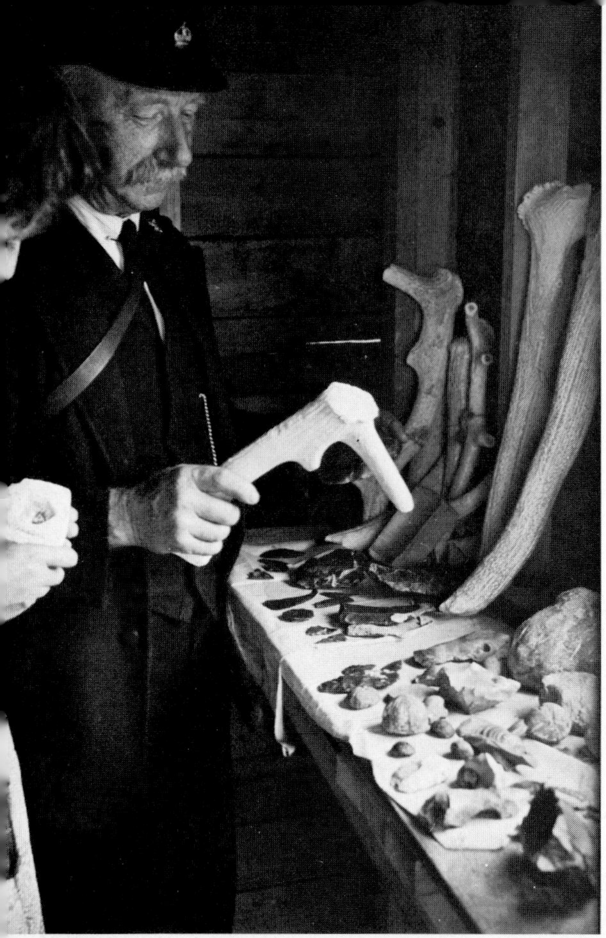

In Mr Mitchell's hut,
Grime's Graves

Galleries in the flint
mines, Grime's Graves

Flint knappers at work,
Brandon

Monument to Susan Blythe,
Swaffham Church

Left: Angel roof, Swaffham Church

Above: The ruins of Roudham Church

The Nave, East Harling Church

cultivation and building, whether of a temporary or permanent character, are the causes of the decline in the numbers of stone-curlews during the past twenty or thirty years.

Breckland is one of the few parts of England where this fine bird is still to be found. It was first noticed in the district in 1674 when Sir Thomas Browne, who was resident in Norwich, killed a specimen near Thetford and made a pen-and-ink drawing of it which can now be seen in the Natural History Museum. The stone-curlews make their way to Breckland from North Africa, arriving towards the end of March and departing again early in October. They lay their eggs, two of them, in a hollow scraped in the sand. I have only once seen a nest; it was near Santon and I should never have noticed it if I had not been searching for flints, my eyes fixed upon the ground, for the eggs were only distinguished by their perfection of shape from the flints and pebbles among which they rested. They were the colour of stone, spotted and marbled with dark brown. One egg was lighter in colour than the other and the small end of the first was placed against the large end of the second. The depression in which they were deposited was so broad and shallow that it could have been attributed to the shifting character of the sandy surface of the heath. But photographs show that the stone-curlew will often make a narrow, deeper nest, lined with a few blades of dried grass.

The resemblance of a flint-strewn breck to the seashore explains the presence on some of the heaths of the Ring Plover, some thirty or forty miles from its customary haunts. The bird nests on derelict brecks, utilising, like the stone-curlew, a hollow in the sand, which perfectly camouflages its sand-coloured eggs. Sometimes the nest is lined with tiny stones, and from this habit the Ring Plover derives the name by which it is known in Breckland, stone-hatch. A century or so ago these birds were described by the naturalist, J. D. Salmon, as "very abundant" in the neighbourhood of Thetford. W. G. Clarke, who with his deep feeling for locality combined such remarkable

precision that he could always tell how many varieties of
birds or wild flowers there might be on one particular stretch
of heath, reported that in 1925 there were not more than four
hundred pairs of Ring Plovers in the whole of Breckland. Only
a skilled observer, such as I cannot pretend to be, could make
an accurate census of inland-breeding stone-hatches today, but
their numbers have certainly decreased very sharply and the
bird is seen more rarely than the stone-curlew. I have heard its
haunting dissyllabic note on the heaths of West Stow and
Cavenham, between Mildenhall and Elveden, on the Mundford road not far from Thetford and down by the Nar near
Castle Acre, but my only opportunity of seeing the bird at close
quarters occurred on a warren between Hilborough and South
Pickenham. It was summer, towards evening; the trunks of a
group of pines glowed vermilion against a sky of clearest green.
On either hand, far distant, was the abrupt horizon of the open
heath. It was a day of great heat and the fire and splendour of it
were reflected in clouds of butterflies, in the patches of scarlet
and purple made by poppies and flowering grasses and in dazzling stretches of stony breck speckled with the blue of viper's
bug-loss. The track across the warren passed through a little
copse, a tangle of hawthorn and crab-apple trees set about with
pines. In the heart of this thicket, like a fairy-tale house, a trim
cottage stood upon a pocket handkerchief of a lawn. It was of
flint with its pretty Gothic porch and arched windows outlined
in red brick. Creamy roses climbed the walls and a neat trellis
of sweet-peas divided lawn and trees. As I watched, a red-faced
man wearing gaiters and carrying a gun stepped out of the neat
door and completed the likeness of the enchanting scene to a
sporting print of the early nineteenth century. Just beyond this
copse I noticed the footprints of some fairly large bird in the
sand. I thought they might belong to a stone-curlew, but I paid
them scarcely any attention, for my imagination was still engaged by the little house and at the same time I was distracted
by the unexpected appearance of a stock dove from the depths
of a rabbit burrow. Without knowing it I must have passed

quite close to the nest of a stone-hatch, for two black and white birds showed suddenly just above me and began to circle about me, one of them uttering a short, melancholy, mellow whistle which I recognised with an agreeable and totally unwarranted sensation of achievement.

On that day I had been bicycling over open country for about five hours; I had crossed two high roads, but except for the sportsman I had seen no one. Despite plantations, training camps and attempts at cultivation there are few places where the sense of primeval apartness is stronger than in Breckland. The warrens of Stanford and Bodney, Tottington and Gooderstone, Eriswell High Warren, parts of Roudham and Brettenham Heaths, Hargham and Snetterton Heaths, Thompson Common, Lingheath and vast stretches about Icklingham and West Stow, and far-reaching intervals here and there among the plantations all over the district, are still virgin wilderness. They are barren and useless, but therein lies their significance. They stand aloof from the fevers of so-called progress. On the heath the routine, the cares of everyday life fall away before the consciousness of the deep, eternal bond which links man and nature. The sights and sounds of the wild may sometimes kindle a feeling of ecstasy, but even more to be cherished is the rare sense it inspires of permanence and complete rest.

The aspect of the heath is continually changing, not only with the seasons but with every hour. I was once on Lakenheath Warren early on a July morning. I seemed to feel a surge of elemental forces in the chorus of blackbirds, skylarks and pipits, in the joyous burst of a single thrush from the top of a pine, in the flash of wheeling lapwings, in the flinty call of a whinchat, in the scent of thyme, in the sweetness of the air, in the glow of the newly risen sun on a pale white rose. The day promised much. But before noon the landscape was no longer recognisable. The blue sky of summer had become leaden, the birds were silent, a cutting north wind was sweeping unimpeded over the heath. Colour was gone from the warren; bugloss, sorel and hound's tongue were swallowed up in drab, hostile greyness. The lichen-moss, which is as common on the heath as bracken and dry, stiff grass, suddenly became more prominent than all the other vegetation. Its pallid, duck-egg green reflected the steely glitter of the light and there was something nightmarish in the way its spongy surface received and retained the impression of my footsteps.

Spring in Breckland is less spectacular than any other season. Frost lingers long and when it relents not a single primrose or cowslip brightens the open heath. But acre after acre is blanched by the tiny, delicate flowers of the whitlow grass and nowhere have I seen such a profusion of crab-apple blossom and such hoary, twisting trunks. There is an avenue of them near Rushford, and on the heath beyond the village a group of these trees, growing to a height of thirty feet, so richly billow from top to bottom with pale pink flowers that even Samuel Palmer's apple blossom cannot rival them.

As the year wears on so the splendour of the heath unfolds. The bracken grows taller and sturdier until it is like some tropical jungle of tree-ferns through which it is difficult to pass; mile upon mile of heather breaks slowly into flower. Even roads white with dust and ferny glades reverberating with the disquieting hum of mosquitoes cannot temper the pleasures of high summer. The dry intense heat burning the sand, so that it is impossible to put a bare foot upon it, is intoxicating; and as it reaches its August climax, so the heath takes on the colours of fire. There is a warren near Swaffham on the edge of a little wood, not a State forest, but a haphazard, ragged belt of pine, beech and fir, which at that time of year is burnished to the horizon with the yellows of ragwort, bird's-foot refoil, lady's bedstraw, sickle medick, flixweed, mignonette, stone crop and hawkweed. Near the trees restharrow, rosebay and the seashore flower, the pink catchfly, make a carpet of rose and purple. It is as though the earth would rival the carmine and gold of the summer-morning sky. Shimmering heatwaves tremble upon that sea of colour and the distant brow of the warren, usually so clear, looks vague and indistinct.

Such moments are the culmination of all that is predicted by the first bracken frond, the first breath of spring; and to me the mystery and excitement of Breckland have then reached their height. But in autumn the pageantry of the heath is such that not even the most casual eye could witness it unmoved. The heather is in full bloom, but though it sometimes covers immense stretches, as on Roudham Heath, it is never so unvaried an expanse of purple as to seem obviously pictorial and leave the imagination cold. The brilliance of Breckland heather is everywhere enhanced by contrasts, by the lion-brown slope of a breck, by blowing tresses of yellow bents or by great patches of golden or vivid green bracken. The heather is at its most splendid on the more exposed warrens, where the air is laden with its delicate scent; and I always think it must have been some Breckland heath which drew tears of joy from Linnaeus when he visited England and saw for the first time a wild moor purple with ling. But the most striking images of autumn are encountered on heaths such as Snetterton and Hargham, clothed largely by bracken, pines, hawthorns, larch and birch. By the end of summer the bracken has grown in sheltered places to incredible proportions. Its curling branches spread high above a man's head, dyed gold and russet, sometimes pressing so closely together that not even a rabbit, it seems, could pass between them, at other times opening out into green dells where no human foot has ever trodden. Thorn trees and the trunks of pines are swathed by the yellow leaves and scarlet berries of bryony and in the midst of the bracken a young birch burns like a flame. Such is the scene by a narrow road near Hargham. The nutty smell of autumn fills the nostrils; the whole countryside echoes with the pheasant's cry. The sun, still strong, catches the lightly undulating road so that it winds like a shining, lilac ribbon through the riot of gold, purple and red. There is glint of green against the autumn blaze and a woodpecker, disturbed perhaps from its feast on an ant-hill, moves with wavering flight over the trees uttering its curious, discordant note. In one lonely spot there has been an attempt to cultivate the heath and two men and a woman in a crimson blouse are setting potatoes.

The day soon declines, a thick, milk-white mist rises from the heath, the brilliant colours of bracken and foliage are dimmed. They take on fantastic shapes and it is not difficult now to believe in the spectre known as the White Rabbit which is said to haunt the warrens near Thetford. It has large, flaming eyes and runs with such speed that it can never be caught. Many people have seen it and it always bodes ill. Thoughts of ghosts are encouraged by the appearance of an abandoned training camp. Rotting huts, empty hangars and concrete runways loom dismally out of the mist. The concrete ruthlessly covers an ancient tumulus marked on the map; but distress at such an outrage gives way to confidence in the vitality of the wilderness as the hard surface of the runway is seen to be rent by great fissures and cracks, through which already furze, fern and heather are forcing their way.

As winter approaches, rough squalls attack the giant vegetation of the heath. They tear and batter the tree ferns till they are laid low and their hue has changed to a dull brown or a faded plum. When these dusty colours are streaked with white after the first fall of snow the heath looks like a Chinese landscape. The absence of birdsong emphasises the sense of illimitable space and solitude. I remember a winter day on the warren adjoining Thetford golf course as one of the most impressive I have spent in Breckland. It is an exhilarating place at any time, steeper than most heaths of the district and commanding wide views over the surrounding country. Now, the parti-coloured heath rolled towards the black waters of the Little Ouse and then climbed towards a plantation which showed intensely dark beneath a cap of snow. Beyond were acres of white, fringed again by firs and pines, smoky, strangely regular stains, like distant armies, against heavy clouds. On the farther slope of the river the dead bracken was only lightly powdered, but a tangle of hollies and a row of willows were laden, the glistening burden of each twig clear before the sombre sky.

Every now and then a gust of wind would shake a miniature blizzard from the trees. The silence, like darkness on the heath, was palpable. Nothing interrupted it but the flight of six dazzling swans which skimmed the Little Ouse with a sound like a gale in taut wires. But on the way to Brandon there was evidence of much unsuspected life. The tail-marks of rats could be made out in the snow, a furrow with claw-prints on either side of it showed where a mole had passed, the three-pronged indentations of the pheasant linked by a thin line recurred again and again, and rabbit tracks crossed one another in all directions. Under the brow of a hill twenty or thirty of these creatures sat with pricked ears, dark and motionless.

The rabbit is king of the heath, the animal that flourishes best in Breckland. The very aspect of the warren is due in part to the rabbit's activities. Where he has cropped it, the heather is as green as grass and so short that it rarely blooms; he keeps the turf smooth and springy, he levels the moss which lines heathland tracks; he tunnels into every slope, kicking out the sand with his strong hind legs and considerably helping the action of windstorms upon the light soil. Breckland conies have always been reckoned a table delicacy and their fur was considered marketable as far back as 1573, when an entry in the Household Book of Sir Thomas Kytson of Hengrave Hall mentions the purchase for three shillings and threepence of six "Black Coney skins to my Mrs Night gown".

Though rabbits so greatly abound in the district, the penalties for taking them were, as readers of Mr Michael Home's Breckland novels will remember, until comparatively recently, very severe. Solitary confinement, hard labour, whipping and transportation were common punishments during the last century. A man named Cross was sentenced in 1805 to six months' imprisonment and to be publicly whipped at Brandon for stealing two rabbits from Wangford Warren; in 1813 Robert Plum was transported for seven years and his friend, Rush Lingwood, aged only eighteen, was doomed to two years' hard labour for taking a coney from a trap at Hockwold. A French visitor to

Breckland in 1784 was astonished at the numbers of rabbits he saw, but said they could not be shot at or caught since the penalty was so disproportionate to the prospect of gain that none would be willing to take the risk. The hazards of poaching at the close of the Victorian era and the excitement of snaring rabbits or of trapping them at night with net, stakes and ferrets are described by Mr Home in *Spring Sowing* and in *God and the Rabbit*. Another way of catching and killing rabbits, formerly much used, was to trap them in pits, known as tipes, a word of Yorkshire origin, current otherwise only in Breckland. These tipes were circular, about eight feet in depth and lined with flints so that the animals could not burrow their way to freedom. An iron, swivelling cover enclosed the pit and upon this enticing bundles of hay would be placed. But no sooner did a rabbit attempt a nibble than he would be cast down into the tipe.

In some parts of Breckland, where the land is especially poor, farmers cultivate rabbits as their chief produce. From February to September the creatures are left in peace, treated like domestic animals, carefully fed, even during the coldest months. Then the farmer, aided by men who live on the warrens and know the ways of rabbits intimately, goes out day after day with nets, ferrets and lurchers, pursuing tracks which so greatly resemble one another and are so interlaced that only the expert can distinguish them or follow one without getting lost. To the warrener each has its own character and he will give them such names as the Cross Roads, the Highwrong Road, the Hay Track or the Dogfold Road. The rabbits are sold for table or sent to Brandon, where for a century and a half Lingwood's hat and fur factory has been a centre for the manufacture from hare and rabbit skins of felt hats.

It is easy to understand how a legend such as that of the White Rabbit came into being in such a district. But there are other tales told of the Breckland heaths. Tutt's Hill, a barrow between Thetford and Euston, is the spot where a traitor was hanged. Tutt was a Saxon shepherd who disclosed to the enemy

Danes an undefended way into Thetford across the river. He had been promised a reward "beyond his highest expectations" and the reward, after the town had been taken, was death. Some poachers once killed a gamekeeper on Croxton Heath, and put the corpse in their cart along with the rabbits they had trapped. They took the road to Thetford and before long passed a sand-pit, which seemed to be a convenient place to hide the dead man. As they were lifting him out of the cart he spoke and swore to haunt them forever more. The men set on him again, silenced him for good and buried him hastily in the sand. Since then a hearse, coffin and bearers rise up at midnight out of the pit, travel slowly down the road and turn in a field gate. On Barnham Common there stands the base of a massive cross which is hollow and sometimes filled with water. It is said that once there was a plague in Thetford and no traveller might enter or leave the town until he had washed his money in this basin.

2. ANCIENT TRACKS

In Crome's majestic painting of Mousehold Heath, the ghost of a track can be discerned curving across the swelling turf. That rutted path, accommodating itself so perfectly to the mood of the land, lends a touch of humanity and intimacy to a scene which might otherwise intimidate the spectator. So in Breckland the fearsomeness of the wilderness is mitigated by innumerable trackways, comforting reminders of an age-long pact between man and nature. Many of them were probably used by the Neolithic people. Such are the Pilgrim's Path, Six Tree Road and Seven Tree Road near Icklingham and the Shaker's Road, Wangford. These tracks can each be followed for but short distances; their ends and their beginnings have been obliterated and nothing can be said with certainty of their origin. But Breckland is still crossed by three major prehistoric roads, each of which can be traced for many miles. There is no better way of becoming acquainted with the humour and structure of the region than to pursue these green or sandy tracks, often losing the thread in a plantation, often obstructed by thickets of bramble, dog-rose, sloe and hawthorn, but always conscious of the feet that shaped the path thousands of years ago, always rejoicing in the remoteness of the ancient highway from the traffic of modern, metalled roads.

The Icknield Way, a famous national road, one of the greatest prehistoric roads in the world, first claims attention. It links the east with south-west England and, according to the *Introduction to the Study of Local History and Antiquities* by Jordan and Morris, was the means of communication between Grime's Graves and Avebury and Stonehenge, the men of Wiltshire obtaining their flint implements from the Brandon knappers. Robert Plot, a seventeenth-century antiquarian, was among the first to substantiate the tradition that the Way was utilised, though not remade by the Romans. The road is generally thought to have been named after the Iceni:

> As Icning, that set out from Yarmouth to the East,
> By the Iceni then being generally possest,
> Was of that people first term'd Icning in his race,
> Upon the Chiltern here that did my course embrace.

But John Aubrey referred to the Way as *Ychen*, meaning Upper or Oxen.

It is by no means simple to locate the Way where it enters Breckland at Cavenham. There is a confusion of tracks in the district, each of which is pointed out by inhabitants as the prehistoric road, and each of which is marked by barrows of the Neolithic and Bronze Ages. The Way runs over Cavenham Heath and apparently crosses the River Lark at Lackford Bridge, though it is difficult to distinguish it from two other ancient tracks which met the river, one at Temple Bridge, the other opposite Icklingham All Saints' Church. This quiet village of whitewashed, thatched cottages, its neighbour Icklingham St James and all the surrounding landscape are steeped in the atmosphere of the past. Grass-grown tumuli mark the courses of the prehistoric tracks and the sandy soil is rich in flint implements. Near the great earthen banks above the Lark valley, which may have been thrown up when the Way was constructed, I once picked up a fine-pointed tool after a search of not more than a quarter of an hour. There is every sign that this lonely spot was once a scene of lively activity. Not only Neolithic people passed this way: it was later a busy Roman centre. The Roman tiles in the chancel floor of Icklingham All Saints' Church came from the villas, many of whose foundations have been excavated, to the east of the village. There was an extensive Roman cemetery hard by, from which stone and lead coffins containing skeletons have been recovered together with terracotta fragments. The discovery of coins of Probus and Crispus scattered about in the cemetery indicates that most of the interments must have taken place early in the fourth century.

Long after villas and cemetery had crumbled into the sandy soil the ancient tracks were still in use. There is a reference in a description of the Liberties of Thetford of 1585 to "Lackefordeweye alias Salter's Way", alternative names for the Icknield Way, and until the close of the seventeenth century, when the Little Ouse was first bridged along the main road from Elveden, the Way remained the chief if not the only entrance into Thetford. When it was no longer used as a public highroad, the Way was traversed by cattle-drovers whose flocks and herds were conspicuous features of the landscape before the introduction of cattle trucks and quick railway transport.

Now there is no sign of human life on the green track which, leaving all uncertainties at the river bank, climbs the ridge above the Lark valley and snakes its way towards Shelterhouse or Sheltereye Corner. Every step along the close-cropped turf seems to lead both deeper into the country and farther back in time. Here and there bracken, furze and heather pierce the grass, poor stunted growths that seem to have been pressed down by the feet of the past. After passing across high heathland the Way enters a sombre plantation. Regular shafts of light slant between the evenly spaced conifers and illuminate the serrated leaves of brilliant ferns. Where the golden rays quiver on the high tree-tops they make rainbows in the spiders' webs. Livid fungi line the path and a pair of stockdoves glide noiselessly between the tall, straight trunks. The scene is more artificial than any landscape garden and in so theatrical a setting there would be nothing surprising in an encounter with the headless rider supposed to haunt the Way between this point and the river. He is the ghost of the Archbishop of Sudbury, who was beheaded and left lying near the Lark by followers of Wat Tyler. Nobody dared to remove the corpse for burial and thus it can never find rest.

Soon the Way meets Weatherhill Heath, and still running along the edge of the plantation, but commanding views over to Berners Heath on the other side, it reaches the Wordwell road at Shelterhouse Corner, known also as Elveden Gap because the Way formerly cut here through a parish boundary bank. Between the Wordwell road and Marman's Grave the Way is a wild, partially obscured path, a meeting-place for rabbits seldom disturbed by the tread of a human foot. Straggling hawthorn branches push back the traveller, brambles clutch at his ankles, hillocks of blown sand matted with sandsedge confuse his sense of direction. The black and white plumage of magpies glitters above ragged bushes of elder and dog rose. The noble sweep of heath and breck on either hand, unbroken by hedges or boundary stakes, can scarcely have changed since the Way was made. Where it reaches the edge of the Elveden estate, fringed by gigantic pines and oaks, the track grows smoother and begins to incline very gently towards the road from Barnham to Elveden. A stone marks the lonely crossing and the place where Marman is buried. His identity is unknown. According to one tradition he was a suicide, according to another he was a gamekeeper called Mar, beaten to death by poachers. There could hardly be a more fitting spot for either deed.

From Marman's Grave to Thetford the Way cannot easily be

followed, but it approaches the town opposite the gasworks. The point where it once met the Bury road is marked by a mound said to be the grave of a pirate called Chunk Hervey. The buccaneer retired to Thetford with a fortune and might have become a respected churchwarden if a former companion had not blackmailed and betrayed him. Chunk was executed and buried in this place and from the stake driven through his heart there sprang a magnificent pine which was a landmark until it fell during the last century.

Fording the Little Ouse at Nun's Bridge, once called Incelland Bridge, the Way passed under the shoulder of Castle Hill and then is thought to have forked north-east and north-west. The north-eastern branch can be followed along what is now Green Lane, towards Kilverstone. Hoary elder trees and stunted firs border the deeply rutted, sandy track and it passes a little clearing which in early summer is one of the most poetic places in Breckland. It is covered with the finest grass and with beautiful starry mosses and it runs down to a disused pit, a dark confusion of bushes and nettles. On two sides the clearing is screened by hedges of carmine-coloured wild roses growing in so orderly a manner that it is hard to believe they owe nothing to art. The flowers blossom with an abundance I have never found elsewhere and, long before they can be see, heavy perfume betrays their enchanting presence.

The track peters out before long, and though a row of hawthorns in a field between Green Lane and Roudham Heath may indicate the direction in which the Way once went, there is nothing to prove it.

A map of 1842 shows what appears to be the north-westerly branch of the Way leading through Croxton Park across the Drove road along by West Tofts Plantation to Stanford. Today the track is lost until it reaches the edge of the Plantation. There it passes between earthen banks, one of them planted with gnarled old hawthorns and later with oaks, which give the scene the picturesque character of one of those rutty lanes painted by Ruisdael or Hobbema. The resemblance to a Dutch landscape is soon enhanced by fringes of alders and beds of whispering reeds when the Way, after passing an isolated farmhouse called Bagmore, descends into a marsh and crosses a narrow brick bridge over a dyke.

At Stanford it is one with the metalled Watton road for a few yards, then branches left to ford the Wissey and to run by Buckenham Tofts Park until it merges into a track shown on modern maps as the Smugglers' Road. Here, over Bodney Warren, the Way is raised above the level of the surrounding country; and here again the traveller is vividly conscious of its antiquity. The sense of contact with the past is quickened by the iron-hard quality of the track. Now deserted, it has been pressed by such countless feet in bygone ages that not a century and more of disuse, of wind and rain have availed to loosen the soil. The spiked, tortuous shapes of thorns and gorse, starting up here and there in the bleak landscape, speak also of the past. To the imagination they are more telling symbols of a vanished world than the Bronze Age barrow known as Man Hill which casts its shadow athwart the Way. Beside them the smooth contours of the tumulus seem no more aged, no less familiar than the distant outline of Bodney's little church on its artificial mound. There is no softness in the scene except where the Wissey valley threads the brecks, and the only sound echoing through the waste is one which may have been heard by the prehistoric makers of the Way, the cry of the stone-curlew.

As the road slopes down to the river once more it becomes hollow as though worn by all the traffic which passed along it to one of the most frequented fords in East Anglia. Immense oaks grow on the western side of the path, one of them so great of girth that five persons with outstretched arms can only just encircle it. Plank and handrail bring the traveller safely over the water and the Way then rises steeply to cross another fork of the Wissey and to meet the main road near Hilborough. A modern road follows the course of the Icknield Way from Hilborough to Cockley Cley, metalled except for one short, grassy interlude. This road is high and breezy, overlooking

Gooderstone Warren and dark patches of pine. The grass on either hand, closely shaven by the rabbits, is studded with thyme, sage and yellow bedstraw. Scarcely perceptible, flint-dotted tracks run in all directions over the heath and the iridescent summer plumage and waving crest of lapwings continually catch the eye as pairs of these noble birds wait motionless on the ground for some sequel to the unwonted noise of footsteps.

The Way encounters yet another stream at Cockley Cley, a tributary of the Wissey, where black and white cows stand half hidden by luxuriant growths of meadowsweet, willowherb, blue rushes and burdocks. No sooner has this pastoral scene been left behind than the eye is delighted by another change. Passing to the east of Cockley Cley church, the Way climbs a hill and skirts an open pit where flints were once quarried. A blue and lilac summer sky accentuates the rich ochre of the pit and the pallor of a cornfield above it. Great white-coated flints, like the ancestral forms of sea-lions, lie on the floor of the quarry and overhead clouds of sandmartins swoop and scream, then vanish into a honeycomb of little tunnels in the pit walls.

The direction of the Way is north towards Beechamwell and Narford, where it leaves Breckland to run by Gaytenthorpe, Hillington, Flitcham, Shenborne and Sedgeford to the coast at Hunstanton. As the confines of Breckland are reached, heath and plantation begin to yield to farming land and the track is interrupted by several main roads and once by a railway. But the consciousness of its age persists. It lingers in the tangled roots of a great thorn near Beechamwell, gathering track and bank in a sprawling, knotted net; and it becomes tangible in the strange object known as the Cowell Stone, a glacial boulder bursting from the soil at the corner of the Long Plantation. Most of its bulk is hidden beneath the earth's surface, so that it is like a terrestrial iceberg.

This part of the Way is mentioned three times in the Harleian Roll A10 in the British Museum, a document of the time of Henry IV. There it is described as "Pedderysty alias dicta Saltersty". On the map of 1842, already quoted, the track is marked as "Peddar's Road Round". There seems to be some confusion between the Icknield Way and Peddar's Way, which from Narford to the sea run close and parallel to one another. But whereas the Icknield Way was a national route, Peddar's Way belongs only to East Anglia, crossing Norfolk and Suffolk in a south-easterly direction from the coast at Holme. Very little is known about it except that it was used by prehistoric man and was adapted and improved by the Romans. That the conquerors of ancient Britain were not the first people to construct straight roads is proved by the undeviating course of Peddar's Way. A glance at a map shows the track, broken though its continuity now is, running in a dead straight line across Breckland from beyond Castle Acre to Blackwater on the Little Ouse near Thetford.

Though it is straight, no road could be less monotonous and its original character is more strongly felt than that of the Icknield Way because, except where it passes through Castle Acre and skirts Great Cressingham, it avoids all human habitation, and because its course is so fixedly set towards the south-east it clings more closely than either of Breckland's other two prehistoric tracks to every rise and fall in the level of the land. Peddar's Way is green or sandy for most of its length and bounded by one and sometimes two grassy banks, shaded now by a group of thorns, now by pines, cloaked in white bryony. Like the Icknield Way, it leads the solitary pedestrian directly into the heart of the past. Two of the most impressive sights it has to show are an enormous barrow near Thompson and another barrow in the neighbourhood of Little Cressingham, shaped like a shallow, upturned bowl. This barrow was opened in 1849 and contained a male skeleton, a grooved bronze dagger and the decayed remnants of its wooden handle, a flat bronze dagger, a necklace of amber beads and three small boxes of thin, gold plate which were strikingly similar to Aegean work. The report written at the time of the excavation amusingly reflects the preoccupation of the period with the subject of phrenology; it states that "the skull was remarkably thick and, speaking phrenologically, displayed a large development of the animal passions, as also 'caution' and 'love of approbation'."

Despite the fascination of such speculations the Way confronts the traveller not so much with a vision of prehistory as with a glimpse of medieval England. In the month of May, when Breckland's late spring has sown the path with pale blue forget-me-nots, white starry chickweed, pink vetch and the hairy grey foliage of the cudweed, when thorns are breaking into blossom and "small fowles maken melodye", it is as though the freshness of Chaucer's world has never passed away. The landscape on either hand, unlike so much of rural England, bears scarcely a trace of either the influence of the picturesque or of enclosure. Only weather and season bring change to the aspect of the heath and, where the land is cultivated, the great hedgeless fields look like the open fields of pre-enclosure agriculture. Woods, whether they be native to the scene or the new forests of our own century, now and then accentuate the horizon and give strength to the illusion of the Middle Ages when forests divided manor from manor. One of the few buildings within sight of the Way as it passes above the hollow enfolding Great Cressingham is a house which seems the embodiment of some Romantic poet's dream of medieval England. It was built in about 1545 by John Jenny, whose initials together with a capital E for his wife Elizabeth figure cospicuously in the mingled Gothic and Renaissance ornament which over-spreads the whole upper storey of the surviving front. So rich are the traceried panels of moulded brick and terracotta that the little façade resembles a piece of rose-red tapestry suspended against the clear Norfolk sky. A pine sets off the warm brick, a tangled hedge dividing the house from the muddy, dung-strewn, deeply rutted track by which it is approached. A fair, ragged boy appears in the lane driving two sows before him and completes the resemblance of the scene to a medieval illumination.

Flocks of sheep are still driven along the Way near Castle Acre, as they must have been for hundreds of years, but the pastoral character of Peddar's Way is nowhere so apparent as when it approaches Thompson Water, though this exquisite lake is artificial and was not constructed until 1847. In summer the path is silvered over with camomile which spreads out in large patches over fallow fields already bright with poppies and with viper's bugloss. Peacock butterflies, disturbed in their antics, flutter nervously ahead of the traveller or alight in a panic almost under his feet. Young partridges flee at his coming, though they ignore a scurrying rabbit. Through the leaves of a hedge of crab-apple and maple shines the water. A skein of wild duck whirs overhead. The birds hasten to meet their own perfect reflections and for a moment, as with gentle splash they alight, the immaculate surface is wrinkled. Then it becomes again the smooth mirror of sky, wood and fields, so smooth that it is difficult to distinguish reality and image and a sandy path on the far bank seems to lead down into a green country in the heart of the lake.

When Peddar's Way reaches Wretham and Roudham Heaths it encounters much military traffic and its character, which depends so much upon silence and solitude, is lost. But there is a spot on its course near Illington where the rare Spanish catchfly still grows untrammelled and in such profusion that it gives the impression of a thick crop of hay. Close by are three hollows, one of which is known as Thieves Pit. It was here that robbers, who many years ago broke into Illington Hall, left their horses, reversing their shoes to foil possible pursuers. The district is called Roudham Scutes, a local word for "skirts".

On Brettenham Heath, used for bombing practice and clamorous with the noise of aircraft, the track is faint and overgrown, but as it slopes down to the Thet and Brettenham village it re-assumes for a moment its original guise. On one side it is shadowed by giant pines, on the other cornfields and pasturage roll away to banks of trees. Four brick and flint cottages, the only habitations which stand directly on the Way, mark the beginning of an even steeper incline, at the foot of which a church, a few thatched dwellings and stables and grazing cattle emerge from a bower of willows and water-meadows.

The Way loses itself among these watermeadows. It is shown on a map published in 1836 as a clear path going straight across the Thet to the Little Ouse, which is traversed by the Blackwater ford. But it can only now be partially traced, its probable course indicated by the position of several tumuli near the river and of an earthen bank beyond the water.

Where it crosses Roudham Heath and the railway line, Peddar's Way meets another prehistoric track, the Drove. This road is confined entirely to Breckland and was apparently constructed to join Peddar's Way with Hockwold and the Fens, at that time an island-dotted morass. Until the advent of railways the Drove, like the Icknield Way, was constantly used by shepherds and herdsmen bringing their animals from the fen country into Norfolk. Thus it has fallen into a state of neglect comparatively recently; yet, except where it forms the highway between Hockwold and Weeting, it is no more than the roughest sandy lane scarred by indistinct wheel-marks, and it is hard to believe that the air along its lonely course was ever stirred by human bustle.

That course reveals the wildest aspects of Breckland. Through mile upon mile of heather and bracken, over stony brecks and through the indigo recesses of plantations, the Drove passes close to Grime's Graves and brings the traveller to those other spectacles of the district, Fowlmere, Langmere and Ringmere. Both Peddar's Way and the Icknield Way are varied by streams, cultivated lands and flowering trees. The Drove encounters only one tiny brook on the outskirts of Weeting and that is sometimes dry. From the sandy, barren slope of Bromehill it yields a view of the Little Ouse valley, and for about half a mile after it has crossed the Thetford–Watton road the track is bordered by a low hedge. But all the rest of its fourteen miles lie through unrelieved bracken, heather and dismal pines.

At one point the Drove recalls medieval England. It is at Weeting where it runs through the park and passes close to Mount Ephraim. In the plantation here there lies a broken fourteenth-century cross of Barnack stone. According to Blomefield, pilgrims on their way to Walsingham used this part of the Drove, which was known as Walsingham Way at that time, and here "was formerly a stone cross, now broke into two pieces, commonly called the Stump Crosses".

But the fragments are not only embedded in nettles, they are overshadowed by two exceptionally large, ditch-encircled barrows defying the cross, asserting the pagan creed of the prehistoric roadmakers.

At present the last part of the Drove is ruined by the continual passage of tanks. Whoever wishes to savour the true atmosphere of this ancient road, strewn, especially in the parish of Santon, with Neolithic implements, and still wearing for most of its length its primeval appearance, should not venture farther than the place where it runs between Fowlmere and the tiny, crater-shaped mere known as the Devil's Punchbowl. There the spirit of prehistory is strong. As evening falls, mists rise from the circular pool and take on the shape of a white crown, a moorhen picks her way along the pebbly shore, the broken branch of a pine groans in a sudden gust, a vole gripped in the talons of an owl squeals with fright and the pale track leads into the dark, furry looking, gently swelling waste as it led three thousand years ago.

3. TREASURE TROVE

Wind blows the loose sands of Breckland hither and thither, burying a necklace lost on the heath a week ago, uncovering a brooch which has not seen the light for fourteen hundred years. The treasure hunter can comb the same strip twenty times and find as much variety in it as if the ebb and flow of as many tides had drained and replenished it. But tides change the nature of all they embrace and the light, dry soil of Breckland preserves unimpaired through centuries every object committed to its care.

Just as no casual visitor to the south-west of Sicily can believe that he has only to look at the broken pottery which lies everywhere on the scorched, ochre-coloured earth to find fragments of the finest Greek ware, so it is hard at first to imagine that relics of vanished cultures lie exposed or but just beneath the surface of the brecks and warrens of East Anglia. The most commonly found treasures are the prehistoric implements already described. But the sand continually yields other relics, sometimes of a spectacular nature. A Saxon bronze brooch of robust workmanship, in the form of a conventionalised leaf with intricate gilt decoration, was picked up at Bridgham a few years ago and at about the same time a farmer of Rushford found a large Saxon urn shaped like a fat bottle and encircled at its greatest width with a row of large round knobs. Coins bearing upon them the word ECEN (Iceni) and occasionally decorated with the figures of horses are not infrequently thrown up by the sand. Relics of the Bronze and Iron Ages are common. Among the many discoveries which have been made, not only by professional archaeologists but by the people of Breckland themselves, may be mentioned the remarkable tankard of the Early Iron Age turned up by the plough at Elveden in 1888. It is adorned with circular bronze disks bearing incised designs like those found on Celtic jewellery. At Saham Toney flint quarriers came upon a fine set of Iron Age horse trappings; and a Middle Bronze Age sword was identified by Mr R. C. Parrott of Weeting about three years ago. It measured over two feet in length and was made between 800 and 200 B.C. A Hockwold man had found it and for some time before Mr Parrott saw it he had been using it to "top" sugar beet. Bronze Age barrows are more numerous in Breckland than in any other area of the same size in East Anglia. Only a few of them have been excavated and there is no doubt that many of the others will one day yield memorable finds. Among the most interesting of the tumuli so far examined was one at Barnham, where

Mrs R. B. Caton unearthed ten urns of fine, simple shape, an Iron Age vase, an Anglo-Saxon sword of iron, a knife, a spear-head, part of a shield and over two hundred flint tools.

Relics of the Roman occupation are always exciting attention in Breckland. It is unlikely that the conquerors established themselves on more than a modest scale in so sparsely populated and barren a district, but in proportion to their numbers more of their belongings have survived unharmed than in regions where the soil is moist and heavy and has been frequently disturbed by building operations. A delicately wrought bronze ceremonial head-dress and two gleaming coronets came to light one Easter Monday on Cavenham Heath. A farm worker at Elveden happened on a pottery vase, quite intact and filled with hundreds of silver coins, as recently as the spring of 1953. Remains of villas have been excavated at Methwold and Stanton, and the discoveries at Icklingham of both a villa and a cemetery have been mentioned in the previous chapter. Fragments of Roman pottery, generally Castor and Upchurch ware, may be acquired by any sharp-eyed person taking a walk along the Drove where it descends Bromehill, and some favoured treasure hunters have happened upon bracelets and tiles in that area.

Objects from the Breckland sands may be seen in the museums of Norwich, Ipswich and Thetford, but the most astonishing of them all is displayed in the British Museum, a treasure so costly and so sumptuous that it has impressed multitudes who have never heard of Breckland. The Mildenhall silver was dramatically discovered in 1942 by Mr G. Butcher, who was working in a field at West Row, not many yards from the site of a small Roman villa. He was tractor-ploughing for Mr Syd. Ford on skirt or "field" land, as it is locally called, land where fens and brecks meet. Mr Butcher was ploughing deep and was using a safety-plug in case of bog oaks. Suddenly the plug snapped and the tractor shot forward, leaving the plough behind. On investigating the cause of the trouble Mr Butcher found that his plough had struck a piece of metal. He called to Mr Ford, who was working nearby, and together the two men unearthed a number of discoloured objects which, as far as they could make out through the grime with which they were thickly coated, appeared to be made of pewter. Mr Butcher was not in the least excited by the discovery, but Mr Ford's imagination was stirred. He carried the objects carefully home to Grove Villa, West Row, and set to work to clean them. Rich ornaments and figures began to emerge and soon the little sitting-room seemed to be filled with gleaming bowls, plates, ladles, spoons and goblets. The most magnificent object of all was a great dish measuring two feet in diameter, adorned with a Bacchanalian frieze, with nereids and sea creatures and, in a central medallion, a full-faced head of Neptune in bold relief. Mr Ford was much taken with the frenzied maidens in their flowing robes, he admired the accurate, academic treatment of features and muscles and he particularly liked the figure of the horned, goat-footed Pan in the outer frieze. The god is portrayed leaping nimbly over a pile of fruit knotted in a skin. Draped over his arms and behind his back is a skin cloak and in his left hand he holds his reed pipe. The Breckland farmer loved his lively, devilish expression and decided he must represent Satan. He kept the dish on his sideboard and enjoyed the company of nymphs and satyrs for about four years. Then one day he invited Dr Fawcett to see what he called his Roman pewter. The doctor at once said that the discovery should be reported. An inquest was held on July 1st, 1946, the Mildenhall silver was declared treasure trove and consequently Crown property; and now Mr Ford can only see his old friend Satan if he makes the journey to London. It says much for his feeling that he is often to be observed in the King Edward VII Gallery in the British Museum.

From its resemblance to a similar but far more damaged hoard of silver, known as the Traprain Treasure, found in East Lothian and now in the National Museum of Antiquities, Queen Street, Edinburgh, the Mildenhall treasure is ascribed to the fourth century. A covered bowl, the lid of which is surmounted by the figure of a triton and adorned with animal figures and human masks, may be of earlier date. It is not known where the treasure was manufactured. The various pieces may have come from different Imperial centres of silver-working. A niello dish, more restrained than the rest, decorated with an incised, formal pattern inlaid with niello, may be of Eastern origin, while some of the objects were perhaps made in Britain. The remarkable condition of the silver may be attributed not only to the chance that it was buried in Breckland soil but that it seems never to have fallen into the hands of barbarian plunderers. It was probably hidden by its owners in an emergency during the troubled years of the later fourth or early fifth century with the intention, never realised, of recovering it at some later time.

The interest of the Mildenhall treasure resides chiefly in its perfect condition and its extent. Aesthetically many of the pieces are disappointing. The principal object, the so-called Neptune dish with its arbitrary design, mechanical and over-naturalistic treatment, is reminiscent of nothing so much as the modern, decadent Lalique ware. A pair of platters ornamented with figures in relief of Pan and a maenad and a dancing satyr and maenad, show immense skill in the technique of casting, but little feeling for design. Not only do the figures bear no relation to the circle which encloses them, but other objects are scattered indiscriminately about the surface of the platters and add nothing iconographically. On the one a water nymph reposes above the main figure while below them an urn rests on a pedestal, a hind sniffs at a tiny snake and a tambourine floats in mid air. On the other a lidded urn hovers above Pan and the maenad, a pair of cymbals lie at their feet among incised plant forms and a crook is tied up in a skin with a bundle of fruit. The most pleasing objects are a number of spoons and the niello dish, which has a beaded rim and an ornamental flange raised slightly above the flat central portion, which is plain but for a circular panel in the centre filled with a pattern in niello of rosette motives enclosed in circles and squares. The spoons are either pear-shaped or oval with long, thin tapering handles. Some of the bowls are charmingly decorated with curling stems and sprouting leaves, while others are plain except for a monogram composed of the initial letters of Christ, which was much used as a sacred symbol in early Christian times. It seems likely therefore that the fourth-century Roman family to whom the treasure belonged were Christian. Two other oval spoons, joined to their elegantly twisted handles by scroll attachments, are inscribed *Papittedo vivas* and *Pascentia vivas* and were perhaps christening presents.

If the Mildenhall silver arouses interest in Breckland as a source of treasure trove of the most glamorous character, the unearthing in 1946 of well-preserved dwellings of Saxon Thetford together with their contents is proof that the sand hides secrets of another but no less fabulous nature. Workmen erecting houses on the New Town Estate on the Elveden side of Thetford suddenly came upon the remans of Saxon huts and countless domestic utensils in perfect condition. Nine hundred years had passed since building operations had last been conducted upon that spot. Photographs of the huts at the time of the discovery and of the excavations which took place immediately afterwards are displayed in the Thetford Museum, and one tent-like hut built of inclining timbers has been reconstructed in Norwich Museum as it was found. It dates from the eighth century and has a rude central hearth about which stand large cooking-pots; smoke from the fire finds its way through an aperture in the roof. In the mud floor are two pits. Among the numerous object found on this Saxon site are several spiky cresset lamps; a big, four-handled storage jar with wavy, vertical lines of decoration like piecrust; a baluster cresset lamp and a three-handled beaker with a spout.

Three years after the uncovering of Saxon Thetford it was necessary to enlarge the new housing estate. As the site had already yielded such remarkable finds, building operations were postponed until further excavations had been made on behalf of the Ministry of Works under the direction of Group-

Captain G. M. Knocker. A number of interesting objects soon came to light: a fragment of a Saxon double-sided iron saw blade, about four inches long and two inches wide, the first saw of the period ever to have been found in England; a gouge, a hammer, an adze and a file; a bone skate; horseshoes; and a large number of pottery bowls, lamps and storage jars. But the most astonishing discovery was made by two workmen, Mr John Wright and Mr William Bailey, who suddenly hit on a hard substance pierced by four apertures, which turned out to be the top of a kiln. It was the first Anglo-Saxon pottery kiln ever to have been excavated. Only an expert could have recognised it at a first inspection. Broken away in parts, encrusted with sand, it looked like some curious, hollow rock. The four flue-holes, regularly placed, were evidence of man's handiwork; and an examination of the interior revealed a sight almost as moving as the deer picks found by Canon Greenwell at Grime's Graves, a wattle and daub lining marked with the finger impressions of the men who had built the kiln. It is not yet understood how the kiln was fired. This rough, un-romantic-looking, yet stirring object has found its way, like the Mildenhall treasure, to London, and is now to be seen in the Science Museum.

The discovery of this kiln was soon followed by the unearthing of two others of the same type. The output of pottery at the end of the tenth century was enormous, and Thetford ware was known all over central and eastern England.

4. BRECKLAND FORESTS

From what has been so far written it is apparent that the present aspect of Breckland depends very largely on the work of the Forestry Commission. The landscape described by W. G. Clarke has undergone so great a transformation since the first State forest was planted in 1922 that, if he could return, he would be unable to recognise some of his favourite haunts. To one who never knew the original Breckland the dusky, monotonous acres of conifers are part of the scene, an essential component of its remote, alien character. Enough has been said to show that these strange forests do not always lack atmosphere. Viewed from the Mundford road after a fall of snow, Thetford Chase lies like a mysterious, smoky cloud across the land, stretching to the horizon, shutting off the everyday world. To enter its silent, nightmarishly repetitive avenues is to step into the typical setting of German and Slavonic fairy-tales. It was in just such a forest as this of endless murky tree aisles and flowerless, needle-strewn earth that the widow's daughter in *Die drei Männlein im Walde* sought in vain for strawberries. It would not be surprising to meet the three dwarfs of that same story in Emily Wood or to come upon the house of the sorcerer, Fitcher, who lived in the heart of just such a dense pine forest and ensnared unwary maidens.

The foreign spirit of the State forests was emphasised in a curious way when one winter's morning I was walking through Emily Wood. The track, deep in snow which showed no trace of animal or human foot, passed through a forest so thick that only the tops of the trees were white. Below, all was dark and lifeless. Every now and then the wind would stir the trees, drawing from them a soft, eerie moan and shaking down from them a light powdering of snow. All at once I saw a figure coming towards me from far down the rigidly straight drove. He was slipping and stumbling in the furrows and holes concealed by the snow, hastening as though pursued. As he hurried nearer I saw that he was dressed in an outlandish fashion, entirely in keeping with his surroundings but quite unlike the attire of any self-respecting East Anglian. Upon his head was a round fur cap coming down over the ears. He wore a leather, fur-lined jacket, open a little at the neck to show a crimson scarf. His baggy trousers of heavy blue tweed were thrust into the tops of calf-high, clumsy boots strapped about his legs. He had a round, red face, small light eyes, prominent cheek-bones and a thick, wide mouth. As we met he smiled and said something in a questioning tone in a language I did not recognise. I spoke to him in English, but he understood nothing. He seemed to have lost his way, so I pulled out my map and showed him the routes to Brandon and to Thetford. But the man shook his head and his persistent smile began to seem a little alarming. As it did not seem possible to communicate with him I turned to continue my way. The man uttered tones of protest and for a time kept at my side repeating his original question in the same uncouth tongue. At last, when he had returned nearly to the point where I had first caught sight of him, he wheeled round and made off muttering and talking to himself, leaving me with the sensation that the un-English atmosphere of the Breckland plantations was far more than visual. I was much exercised by this encounter until, later in the day, I met a forester's wife who told me that the man must have been one of the Ukrainians employed on the Elveden estate. She said they were indeed strange people; they lived wholly on fat bacon.

It is time to ask how the Breckland forests came into being. There are three of these unnatural pinewoods: Thetford Chase, which covers more than 48,000 acres of land in the neighbourhood of Thetford and Brandon; Swaffham Forest, which lies to the north and occupies 4,000 acres; and King's Forest, stretching across 6,000 acres in a southerly direction towards Bury St Edmunds. In all, this forest region involves almost half the district with which we are concerned. The Forestry Commission first acquired land in 1920 from Lord Iveagh which had been part of Wangford Warren; and as one by one many of the great estates were brought by economic pressure into the market, more and more territory was purchased and destined for afforestation. The Downham Hall Estate, the land belonging to Lynford Hall, property from the Croxton Abbey Estate and lands at Methwold were added to the heath leased by Lord Iveagh and eventually formed the immense forest of Thetford Chase, the name having been given to the district in the time of James I, who was particularly fond of hunting there. Mr Francis Allen's Cockley Cley Estate became the nucleus of Swaffham Forest in 1920.

The new plantations were intended to increase the amount of timber produced in Britain so that she should no longer, as in 1920, be compelled to import ninety per cent of her timber requirements. And there was more than practical advantage to be derived from the scheme. Mr W. C. Taylor, writing in 1925 in the *Quarterly Journal of Forestry* (XIX, pp. 192–212), looks forward to the time when forest traditions will be so firmly established in Breckland that the district will witness a renaissance of medieval woodland England, where self-sufficing communities of foresters will thrive in the heart of the woods and son will follow father in the noble profession of forestry.

The initial operations of the Forestry Commission were not such as would inspire confidence in the growth of local tradition. Alder and birch trees in the Little Ouse valley at Santon Downham, and two giant Douglas firs which stood near the mansion formerly occupied by the Duchess of Cleveland and were known throughout the district, were hacked down and the timber sold to clog-makers; and everywhere the natural vegetation of heath and warren, the grasses, mosses, heather and lichen, together with all the bird, animal and insect life, were exterminated by plough and spade. The land was then separated into mathematically defined "compartments", each compartment divided by a grassy ride and each covering a area of about twenty-five acres. Broad-leaved trees would not flourish on Breckland soil and only two kinds of trees lent themselves to the large-scale planting planned by the Forestry Commission—Scots and Corsican pines. Thus, although an official publication of 1925 assured the public that it was not the intention of the Forestry Commission to create a series of hard-outlined, rectangular plantations devoid of relief, that is what has very largely occurred. Only here and there along some of the main roads are the close, coniferous ranks screened by lines of light-leaved sycamores and oaks.

The young trees are raised from seed, sown in nurseries at Harling and Weeting, and planted on the brecks when they have reached the height of about six inches. The chief enemies of the new, tender growths are wind-blown sand and rabbits. Little can be done to protect the trees from a sandstorm, but this danger decreases as the forest areas expand. The forester's method of dealing with rabbits is ingenious and simple enough to merit more than a passing mention. He first drives into the ground rough sawn or cleft stakes and struts about ten feet apart; then from a single strand of barbed wire, strained taut at a height of about three feet, he hangs a small-meshed wire netting. The netting is six inches longer than the posts and the forester turns back the additional length at right angles to the fence and lays it along the ground outside the enclosure, keeping it in position by means of sods. The method has proved more successful than the alternative of burying six inches of netting in the soil.

The Breckland pinewoods are in charge of sixteen foresters, each of whom is responsible for a particular beat, called by its local name, Roudham, Croxton, West Toft, Santon, Downham, High Lodge, Elveden, Didlington, Cranwich, Methwold, Lynford, Hockham, Harling, Mildenhall, Swaffham or Culford. The foresters are in turn controlled by three Forest Officers whose headquarters are at Santon Downham; and under the foresters are foremen and gangers, each of whom is responsible for the work done by the men in his charge. Almost six hundred workers are at present employed in the State forests, many of them foreigners. Foresters and foremen are for the most part trained at Lynford Hall, a Victorian mansion in pastoral ground by the Wissey. Some of the workers are housed in hostels such as the one at High Lodge, but the Forestry Commission has from the beginning established as many men as possible on small holdings, some of which will accommodate several families. The tenants of such holdings are guaranteed not less than one hundred and fifty days' work in the forest each year. The remaining working days of the year he may devote to his garden and to his poultry, pigs and geese. Sometimes houses have been specially built for the forest workers on chosen sites, but generally flint cottages have been utilised which were part of the estates when they were open heathland and privately owned. This development of afforestation, though it does not fulfil all Mr Taylor's hopes, is nevertheless its most interesting and encouraging aspect.

Occasionally the foresters' cottages are so isolated that no tenant will stay, and signs of human habitation in half-cultivated, tiny clearings merely increase the sense of desolation induced by the endless pines. There is such a solitary cottage in the forest which stretches between Elveden and Brandon and I cannot imagine a more melancholy spectacle. After a walk of over an hour through the uneventful, sullen trees a gleam of red shows between the stems and the next instant a squat, ugly little brick house strikes the eye standing in the middle of an untidy, open space. A feeble attempt at gardening has produced a few cabbages by the rough path leading to the front door; the rest of the light, stony soil is hard. A glance at the windows shows a pathetic effort to maintain against overwhelming odds the cosy atmosphere of suburbia. The curtains are all a tasteful shade of cream, scrupulously fresh, and standing between them in three separate windows are a pair of green china frogs and a red and blue gnome with a flower holder on his back, a lamp in the shape of a crinolined female figure and a china ash-tray in the form of a miniature, broken down, black boot peeping from beneath the shiny, long leaves of a bloomless plant in a yellow pot.

On the other hand the houses of foresters at Lynford and Santon Downham are among the most cheerful sights in Breckland. At Lynford the cottages are grouped at the turning which runs through Snake Wood to Grime's Graves. Some are newly built of pale brick with red-tiled roofs, others are old buildings of gleaming flint. In front of each cottage is a little plot as bursting with flowers as any picture-book country garden. Roses and honeysuckle climb about the porches and stocks, sweet-williams, snapdragons and marguerites surge in dense array towards the trim gates, all the more vivid by contrast with the half-grown forest stretching away in ripples of darkest green and blue behind them. Bees hover about the flowers, children play by the sandy track, white sheets swell with the wind on a line in the garden of the end cottage and an air of prosperity and content enfolds the little settlement such as is seldom found in any modern village.

This delightful atmosphere is even more pronounced at Santon Downham, which has been completely transformed by the Forestry Commission and consists at present of a population of about three hundred people, nearly all of whom are wage earners engaged in forestry. A narrow, undulating track slopes steeply towards the village from the main road to Thetford from Brandon. Although Santon Downham is the headquarters of the Breckland foresters, the pine plantations have not here obliterated the former character of the country but form a dusky background to open, pheasant-haunted brecks and carpets of fine grass which were once part of the park of the demolished hall. Magnificent lime trees line the track and through the pale trunks on the left can be seen the glitter of water as the Little Ouse winds through its rushy valley.

The little road leads into the heart of the village, to a green as wide as a common and a church almost hidden in pines. It would be hard to find a pleasanter spot. The grass of the churchyard has been nibbled by rabbits to bowling-green smoothness, its bright colour a welcome foil to the sombre forest, to grey tombstones and to the flint walls of the church. Shallow cherub-heads surrounded by sunflower-like frills gaze from many of the headstones, while one, dedicated to John Gore who died in 1778, exhibits a yardstick and compass, a sun, and weights and measures against a background of mason's boasting; and another, the tomb of Tyrell and Ann Garner, dated 1846, bears an unusually well-carved, bold relief of an urn, draped female figures and swags of roses, acorns, pears and plums. On the south side of the little church is a panel carved with a representation of a lion whose tail bursts into leaf, while tendrils spring from his mouth, apt symbol here of abounding life. The scent of pines mingled with the perfume of lime flowers fills the air and penetrates even to the interior of the church; stockdoves coo softly:

> Coo-oo, Coo-oo
> It's as much as a stockdove can do
> To maintain two;
> But a little wren can maintain ten
> And bring them up like gentlemen;

far away a dog barks, children sport on the green and from the cottages on its edge smoke rises straight towards the cloudless afternoon sky. To complete the pleasure of the moment it is just possible that a pair of those humorous-looking birds, cross-bills or "robin-hawks", may show themselves in the neigh-bourhood. The new pinewoods are said to encourage them, but the bird has always nested in Breckland, especially here at Santon Downham and at West Wretham. Their tameness, which makes them conspicuous whilst they are feeding in the fir woods, caused Sir Thomas Browne to write of them: "The thing most to be noted was that it seemed they came out of some country not inhabited, for that they at the first would abide shooting at them, either with pellet, bow or other engine, and not remove till they were stricken down." They are restless creatures and, like parrots, they climb along the undersides of branches, all the time keeping up a curious low chattering.

Some of the Santon Downham cottages are built of brick, whitewashed, while others, like the forest houses of Scandi-navia, are constructed of wood and painted deep red. They stand high, overlooking the river, the plantations beyond, and a group of older, flint cottages which formerly clustered about the great house. It is a complete community with its own shops, school and places of recreation, and here at least the present has not destroyed the past, but has imbued it with new life. Santon Downham may well produce generations of foresters content to follow in their fathers' footsteps. It is only regrettable that their labours are confined to trees with such limited and unaesthetic possibilities as conifers.

Scots and Corsican pines grow rapidly and after about twenty years it is necessary to thin them out. Two rows in every thirty are removed, woodcutters working singly or in small groups. One man may fell and prepare as many as ninety trees in one day. The timber is loaded on lorries which, owing to the definite pattern followed in selecting pines for felling, can be driven to within twenty-five yards of any cut tree. The vast timberyard by Brandon station is the central depot where the wood is made ready for the consumer. Great piles of poles lie there in hundreds, covering twenty-four acres of land. The thinnest poles are despatched by road to London, there to be made into wall board. Slightly larger trees travel also by lorry to a paper mill in Kent. Other poles are cut into pit props of many different sizes and sent by rail to Midland collieries. Fence posts are made in thousands. The most mature of the Breckland forests are only thirty years old and we should be grateful that the proportion of logs large enough for building purposes is as yet small. The probable use in the future of this unattractive softwood timber for ambitious structures on a large scale cannot be regarded with equanimity.

The danger of fire, which is considerable everywhere in Breckland, nowhere looms so large as in the State forests. In dry weather watch is continually kept over all the thousands of acres of plantations from five look-out towers. Lorries equipped with motor pumps, tools and water supplies are held ready to rush at a moment's notice to any part of the forests. Water tanks and fire brooms are to be seen everywhere in the plantations, the drives between the trees are frequently ploughed to keep the ground clear of inflammable vegetation and all who pass through the wood are reminded at regular intervals to take care with matches and cigarettes. Nevertheless several fires usually disturb the course of each summer and they are among the most alarming, yet fascinating spectacles which Breckland can offer. One August day billowing volumes of dark, threatening smoke could be seen from the road between Thetford and Euston rising above pinewoods in the Elveden direction, dwarfing Lord Iveagh's towering war memorial, a massive urn upon an immense, fluted column which can be seen for many miles around. Several hours later the smoke was as thick as ever and I decided to seek out its source. That morning a cigarette end thrown down by a passing motorist or a spark from an engine had ignited the bracken on the edge of a plantation. It was one of a succession of extremely hot days and the strong, southerly breeze, which often intensifies the heat in East Anglia, fanned the flames towards the trees, where they leaped upon the dry, fallen needles and brittle lower branches. As I drew nearer to the scene of the accident I could see beneath the belching smoke-clouds a line of angry red and I heard a sound as of the firing of hundreds of pistols. Tongues of flame were darting forward to envelop fresh prey and the fire seemed to be advancing in frighteningly regular array, stretching for a distance of about a hundred yards. Crowds of spectators had found their way to the isolated spot and gangs of men were already efficiently at work. Some of them were beating out the flames with fire brooms, struggling to reduce the length of the onrushing line, while in places where the flames were mounting almost tree-high, motor pumps were in action, supplemented a few minutes later by the fire service from Thetford. It was clear that the fire was losing its strength and would very soon be under control, yet the dramatic sight of men moving against the glare in the failing light, the hissing and snapping of the timber, the crash of falling trunks, the blanket of smoke overhead, the darkness and utter silence of the trees which had not yet been attacked, were not soon forgotten. As each pine succumbed to the enemy it stood for a moment sheeted in fire, then, erupting clouds of sparks, it fell. But what struck the imagination most of all was the curiously inanimate quality of the burning trees. They seemed so much less alive than the flames, they seemed to yield themselves as passively to their fate as a long-dried, sawn log. I could not say that the sight of their doom inspired me with any of the fearful sense of destruction conveyed by such a forest fire as that painted by Piero di Cosimo. At the thought of this picture I realised why a close view of the Breckland fire, with all the tension of struggle between man and the most frightening of the elements, moved me less than the distant pillars of smoke. Piero's forest is full of terrified animals, birds and insects rushing in panic from the pursuing flames. Not a rabbit, not a bird, not an insect fled from this fire in Thetford Chase. It was indeed a lifeless victim and the fact that the profitable production of softwood timber was lessened by its fate could not transform a funeral pyre into death by burning.

Although the writer of the Forestry Commission pamphlet, *Thetford Chase*, states that prehistoric Breckland carried forests of oak, beech and Scots pine, other authorities think that, though the district was more wooded then than at later periods, timber was scarce in comparison with other parts of England, and others again consider it extremely doubtful that the region ever bore trees at all. Even Mr W. C. Taylor, who is the most enthusiastic of the advocates of afforestation, insists on the fact that no signs of primitive forest growth have been preserved. The unusual size of Neolithic settlements in Breckland show that the land here must at that time have been relatively clear. The Scots pine, as I have mentioned, was not introduced until the eighteenth century. The shortage of wood in the neighbourhood of Thetford just after the end of the sixteenth century, a period of astonishing building activity in most parts of England, is proved by a royal proclamation of 1604 to the effect that timber was not to be used in the Thetford area for firewood and that no new houses were to be erected unless their walls and windows were made of brick or of brick and stone. It was the scarcity of timber in Breckland which attached special interest to its few natural woods and copses and laid the scene of the legend of the *Babes in the Wood* in Wayland or Wailing Wood near Griston.

Whatever may be said in favour of the State forests and of

forest communities, and however unusual the experiences to be sought in their black depths, it is probable that large forests, and certainly conifers, have never been native to the district. Yet the plantations are spreading week by week, slowly eating up what little of the heathland has been spared by the War Department. Untamed, untouched stretches of country such as the Breckland heaths with their unusual natural life are rare in the confines of Great Britain. They must not be sacrified to utility without a protest.

5. TILLING THE WASTE

My first visit to Elveden, locally called Elden, was during a spell of hard weather when the landscape was blanketed with snow. The road from Thetford, bordered all the way by a path, had the air of an approach to some mansion and estate of more than ordinary importance. The conifer plantations were checked in their dark onrush by many clearings and at one high point, the summit of a long hill, they were quite subdued by a group of towering, gesticulating Breckland pines. The feeble sun struck a gash in one of the trunks and it showed fiery red against the glittering snow. Then the plantations altogether ceased and through tall, pale-limbed beeches great open stretches of white could be seen, cultivated parkland dotted with clumps of oak and cedar.

Yet any conventional notion of hall and grounds, any idea of what lay along the road, which had been formed without some knowledge of the place would fall short of the extraordinary reality. When the village first comes into view it perhaps does not strike the stranger as unusual. It is not indeed built of Breckland flint, but of red brick. Yet the material is typical of Edwardian villages everywhere and the Elveden we see today dates largely from the beginning of the century when it was rebuilt by the 1st Earl of Iveagh. On the day I am describing, the few cottages and the little post office, their steep roofs thickly sheeted in frozen snow, their vermilion walls glowing against the surrounding white and contrasting with the sombre, snow-spotted boughs of enclosing pines, made a picture like a traditional Christmas card. The resemblance was heightened by the goods displayed in the window of the post office which was at the same time a general store. It wanted but a month to the festive season and coloured glass balls; paper bells and paper swags; oranges; transparent bags of boiled sweets; china decorated with a florid azalea pattern; cake ornaments in the shape of Father Christmasses, tobogganing cherubs and robins; tinsel and cottonwool gaily flung back the sparkle of the outside world. The strange appearance of the church, which stood opposite the cottages at the gate of Elveden Hall, hinted, however, at something unexpected. The extravagances of the Gothic Revival are common enough, but the character of Elveden was unique.

It was rebuilt in 1869 by the Maharajah Duleep Singh and enlarged in 1906 by the 1st Lord Iveagh. It was extraordinary that, although the Englishman had been responsible for the present nave and chancel, the building was like an oriental fantasy on the Gothic theme. It was as richly overlaid with ornament as the Great Temple of Bhuvaneswar. Flying buttresses adorned rather than supported the little church in every possible place, clusters of angels were trumpeting from the parapets and the heavily moulded round arch of the entrance was encrusted with rosettes. With the help of Mrs Cornell from the post office, I managed to see the interior, usually locked. It more than fulfilled the promise of the outside. Every conceivable space was covered with minutely detailed decoration. Pulpit, lectern, organ, altar-table, pews and hammer-beams were carved with intricate, lacy designs, capitals and arches derived from oriental models; there were stone panels carved with curious flowers and foliage in low relief; there were angels with long, thin, melancholy Indian faces; and behind them was an alabaster reredos in which the company of boldy carved saints, stretching out on either side and above a representation of the Last Supper, might be taken for rows of nautch girls.

From the church an elaborately vaulted, cloistered way led to a square, flint bell-tower ornamented with complicated flush-work. The tower jutted out into a snow-covered field and what seemed from the tangles of blackened, long unpruned suckers to be a neglected rose garden. To one side was a frozen lake edged by red willow shoots, and facing it across an open expanse varied by elms and a great, leaning cedar was the empty Hall, a parapeted building in the neo-classic style with a central cupola. To the right the sweeping park inclined towards a wooded belt lying upon the purple-hollowed snow like a blue mist. Suddenly the absolute hush of that pale, glittering morning was broken by a rough, resounding cry and close to the bell-tower, running rapidly across the white, appeared a bird as exotic as the church carvings, a magnificent golden pheasant, a creature whose like, unless it were caged and stuffed, could be found nowhere else in England.

The strain was introduced into Breckland by the same Indian prince who so much influenced the character of the church and hall. It was an odd twist of fate which linked his life with that of this remote corner of England. He was heir to the throne of the Punjab and was brought to England as a child after the occupation of his territory by British forces at the end of the Sikh war. In compensation for the loss of his land and the life of an exile he was given an annuity of "not less than £40,000". In 1863 Elveden was in the market, its owner, William Newton, a rich West Indies merchant, having died twelve months previously. The Maharajah purchased it and settled down to the life of an English country gentleman, softened, however, with some of the refinements of the East. Stone lions of Lahore guarded the gateway to his estate and the mansion was transformed. The pediment which adorned the original Georgian façade was torn down; a balustrade was constructed to hide the roof-line; and short wings with bulging parapeted bay windows were flung out on either side of the enriched portico. Of the interior of the former home of the famous Admiral Keppel nothing was preserved but the dining-room, the ceiling of which was decorated with plaques, still in position, commemorating the Admiral's achievements. The rest of the Hall was entirely covered with mirrors and the Prince introduced a massive marble staircase with an ornate wrought-iron railing painted scarlet. Many of the servants were Indian and were dressed in gorgeous livery.

As in the case of the church the 1st Lord Iveagh seems to have been so impressed by the Eastern elements incorporated in the Hall by Prince Duleep Singh that he intensified them. He built a replica of the Maharajah's mansion some yards away from it and then connected the two buildings by a central block one storey higher than the rest of the house and surmounted by a copper dome. This central block was entirely taken up by an "Indian Hall", the details of which were all based on Indian art. It was of dazzlingly white marble, pillared and proportioned like the Taj Mahal, with galleries running all round it and doors of beaten copper. Round the two vast fireplaces which warmed this great chamber the elegant Edwardian house-parties would foregather for which Elveden was famous.

It is only on rare occasions that Elveden Hall may be entered. Lord Iveagh stays in a cottage on his estate when he visits Elveden and except for one wing, which has been converted into flats for workers on the estate, the massive house is deserted. On festive days, however, such as Whit Monday or August Bank Holiday, the marble Hall can be seen in all its splendour and the park is the scene of lively pleasures, sports for the young and sometimes a play, while the old are entertained with flower and vegetable shows, raffles and competitions such as guessing the weight of a piglet or a cake.

Unexpected as is the influence of the Orient in Breckland, there is something more remarkable, if less obtrusive to be seen at Elveden. A map of the whole district published in 1797 shows a surprisingly large area under cultivation. The high degree of exertion and vigilance necessary to farm such soil must have eventually defeated landowners, for soon their tilled fields reverted to open heath. Many attempts to make Breckland productive in the past have failed. Only in our own age, owing to the unwavering determination and outstanding powers of organisation of one man, Lord Iveagh, has the problem been solved.

Part of the Elveden estate is shown as farmland on the map mentioned above, and in 1804 Arthur Young praised the way in which Lord Albemarle, then the owner, was triumphing over the unpromising soil of his property. "The Earl of Albemarle at Elden," he writes, "on a farm of 4,000 acres, which the tenant has at 2s. 6d. an acre, in general consisting of blowing sand, has drilled upon a very large scale, and his Lordship's crops at this commencement of his husbandry have answered his expectations." Lord Albemarle grew a rotation of turnips, barley or oats, seeds for two years, followed by rye or wheat. We learn that he also put down leys of lucerne, the importance of which "on such a soil can never be too highly estimated."

Lord Albemarle's experiment was very successful but he did not pursue it. In 1813, a time of darkest agricultural depression, he sold the property to William Newton. In the century that followed, under Mr Newton, the Black Prince, as he is still affectionately called by Elveden people, and the 1st Earl of Iveagh, the estate was chiefly given up to game, enjoying its heyday as a sporting manor in the Edwardian period, when the reigning monarch was a regular visitor to Elveden. Tom Turner, who in his eighty-sixth year is still head keeper at Elveden, gives a vivid description in his recently published memoirs of the princely sport of those bygone days when "it became a poor day if anything less than 1,000 head were killed the first time over". Farming was undertaken at that time only in so far as it was thought to be "good for the game", though the 1st Lord Iveagh showed that he was not wholly indifferent to agricultural problems by founding at Chadacre, near Bury St Edmunds, one of the first agricultural institutes in England.

When the present owner inherited Elveden it was little more than a vast rabbit warren. In just over twenty years, while preserving part of the estate in its natural state, giving up part to the United States Air Force, and devoting two small areas to the Norfolk Naturalists' Trust and the Royal Society for the Preservation of Birds, Lord Iveagh has reclaimed 8,200 acres of the wilderness, so that they now produce great quantities of excellent grain, sugar beet, milk and meat, while more good farm land is being developed at the rate of five hundred acres a year. Not only has barren sand, proclaimed by the State to be fit for nothing but afforestation, been rendered fertile, but Elveden has become the largest farm in England.

The technical details of how this astonishing feat has been achieved are admirably described in Commander Martelli's book, *The Elveden Enterprise*; they lie outside the scope of this account. Lord Iveagh's interest in agriculture dates from a visit to Canada made in 1910. He was struck by the reluctance of Canadian farmers to employ inexperienced British immigrants and on his return to England he founded a farm on his property at Pyford in Surrey where lads could be trained for agricultural work in Canada and girls who were going there to be married could take a short course to fit them for their new lives. The experiment was successful and stimulated Lord Iveagh's interest in the management of his own farms. Full of original ideas, eminently practical, armed with varied experience, there could have been no one more equal to the challenge offered by Elveden when he succeeded to the estate in 1927. He was sure that the land could be made to produce food, the chief requirements of the dry, light soil being dung and the lucerne which Lord Albemarle had found so helpful.

The first step in the conversion of the land was to restrict the rabbits to the uncultivated heaths by wiring off the acres attached to existing farms. The method of fencing employed at Elveden, it is interesting to note, differs from that used by the foresters in that the bottom of the wire mesh is buried in the ground. Concentrating on the fenced lands, Lord Iveagh found that at Chamberlain's Farm, Eriswell, Church Farm, Icklingham and the Home Farm, Redneck, small dairy herds had been thriving poorly on the scanty indigenous pastures. All the cows were immediately tested for tuberculosis, the infected animals killed and the stock increased by the introduction of Shorthorn heifers, Guernsey calves and calves from Pyrford. The principal ingredient in the cattle food was lucerne hay and about a third of the arable land was devoted to its production. Home-grown cereals, sugar-beet pulp and tops, peas, linseed, mangolds and kale also contributed to the ration. By 1945 such progress had been made that the Elveden Shorthorns gained the Silver Medal of the Eastern Counties Shorthorn Association for an average of 8,493 lb. of milk yielded by seventy-one cows in a year, the highest Shorthorn average in Suffolk. In addition to the dairy cattle there are now more than five hundred beefstock at Elveden.

Thousands of sheep had always eked out a wretched existence on the heaths. Lord Iveagh made drastic reductions in their numbers until there remained two flocks of about five hundred ewes, each in the care of four shepherds. The animals were folded on sugar-beet tops, kale, rye and lucerne; their condition improved out of all recognition and though they have not played so spectacular a part at Elveden as either cattle or crops, they are essential to Lord Iveagh's scheme as scavengers and restorers of the soil's fertility.

The successful breeding and rearing of stock at Elveden depends on the growing of the crops that support them. In addition to lucerne, silage, potatoes, carrots, mustard seed, kale and mangolds, barley, wheat, oats and sugar beet were cultivated with such striking results on the reclaimed land that in the fourteen years between 1939 and 1953 the production of barley was trebled, that of wheat doubled and that of sugar beet increased by one-tenth. The normal procedure at Elveden on freshly broken heathland is to grow two crops of corn, then to enrich the land by folding sheep or cattle on it. After that the regular rotation involves four to five years of lucerne, two of corn, one of sugar beet, one of corn. The operation includes many more processes and far more organisation than this bare statement implies. An analysis of the soil is taken, for instance, each time a fresh tract is ploughed and its basic requirements are carefully assessed.

Various methods are employed for preserving farmyard manure, one of which is to keep the cattle during winter in covered yards, where not only dung is collected, but all the straw produced at the previous harvest is trodden down to make muck; experiments are continually being tried in every branch of farm work, most of them due to Lord Iveagh's lively general interest in farming. His system of making hay on tri-pods, for example, was inspired by a visit to Austria, where the peasants use similar tripods. The advantage of the method is that none of the lucerne touches the ground and the air can cir-culate freely under the tripods. Though the pictorial aspect of such cocks must have been Lord Iveagh's last consideration, it is extraordinarily exciting to see the tall, loose, domed piles of pale green hay regularly dotted about one of Elveden's enor-mous fields against the inevitable distance of pines and conifers.

An inexperienced visitor to Elveden must be chiefly struck by the contrast it presents to the surrounding country. Here a fragile-looking wire net separates a sandy waste, upon which myriads of stones make patterns like those left by receding surf, from a field of rye stretching as far as the eye can see; there the pine formations are abruptly broken by acres of kale among the thick, tall stems of which ewes and well-grown lambs look like the sheep in Giotto's painting at Padua of Joachim among the Shepherds. Here rabbits sport on the plum-coloured heath, divided by only a track and a fence from sleek, tawny cattle nibbling at fresh, succulent lucerne; there a fantastic, bright yel-low machine, driven by one man mounted high above the fore-most massive wheel, digs with countless numbers of cutters into the heather, overturns and buries it, striping the warren with a broad band of brown earth. Here a loose, sandy path meanders between gorse bushes and loses itself in a distance of scrub and pine; there three giant machines, Claus combines, are at work in a field of vast extent, reaping, threshing and tying the straw

in one swift operation, looking like scaly, monstrous insects
with huge antennae, which have come to ravage rather than to
gather the harvest.

In a farm of over eight thousand acres, presenting the diffi-
culties of Elveden, machines are essential. Twenty Suffolk
punches, bred at Elveden, are still in use and occasionally one of
these noble animals may be seen ploughing an undulating,
awkwardly shaped tract and sometimes drawing a harrow between rows of lucerne. But although no modern method is as
effective in getting rid of weeds, as old farm labourers will tell
you, such meticulous husbandry is not generally practical. As
many as fifty tractors and twelve combines are employed on
Lord Iveagh's farm; Thwaites muck-loaders and Massey-
Harris muck-spreaders deal with farmyard manure, a Robot
planter is used for potato planting, Wilder cutlifts, Green crop-
loaders and Paterson Buck rakes facilitate the making of silage,
while the Catchpole beet harvester is put to work on the sugar-
beet fields. The most significant fact which emerges from this
intensive mechanisation, especially to those who, like myself,
feel an instinctive aversion to machines, is that there are twice
as many men employed at Elveden as in 1927. Even allowing
for the increase of acreage under cultivation since that date,
this seems to show that, despite the strongly held belief to the
contrary, the machine does not oust man, but supplements his
powers.

The success of the Elveden undertaking depends very much
upon the skilful management behind it. The entire estate is
organised as a single unit, all farming operations being centrally
controlled. The man who, under the direction of Lord Iveagh,
is responsible for this great farm with its eight thousand acres,
its nine herds of cattle, its two flocks of sheep, its two hundred
workers and mass of machinery, is Mr Victor Harrison, who
was trained at the Chadacre Agricultural Institute. He has been
assisted in his formidable task by Mr Dow, the estate agent,
whose office is in the red-brick cottage next to the post office.
He has been at Elveden since the time of the 1st Lord Iveagh

and his remarkable qualities are reflected in the readiness and enthusiasm with which he has entered into schemes which have changed the estate from the wilderness and game preserve which he first knew into productive land.

There are actually twelve farms on the Elveden Estate and these fall into three groups known as the Home Farms, the Eriswell and the Icklingham Farms. A sub-manager is responsible under Mr Harrison for each of these groups and the daily work of each is arranged by a foreman. Every herd of cattle is cared for by a head cowman working under the manager, the feeding of the animals being the business of the central control. An elaborate system of reports enables Lord Iveagh to keep a complete record of every cow as well as of all the work done on the farms every week.

The housing of all the labourers employed at Elveden is a difficult problem. The Ukrainians, one of whom I met in the plantation on that winter morning, live in the former servants' quarters of the Hall, a little self-contained community with their own Catholic chapel. Other workers live in flats made from the palatial stables, while at least a score of cottages have been built since the war. These cottages have all the amenities of the modern council house, yet the highest rent charged is 4s. 6d. a week. There is no need to point out the significance of such a fact, though in order that it may be properly appreciated it should perhaps be stated that, despite the heavy expenditure involved in overcoming the initial handicaps, Elveden is a profitable concern.

Lord Iveagh's example has been followed by several of his neighbours, and though their achievements are less spectacular than the success of the Elveden undertaking they must command the greatest respect. The work of reclamation carried out at Wretham arouses feelings of special admiration, for it represents not only a triumph over nature but over odds created by man himself. When W. G. Clarke was writing of Breckland thirty years ago, Wretham was a great estate of nearly seven thousand acres whose owner was one of the last of English sportsmen to keep a cast of hawks. The Hall was a fine house in the Georgian style standing in a sweeping landscape garden by the waters of an ancient mere. When the Second World War broke out, Wretham was in the possession of Mrs Rich, renowned as one of the finest women shots in the country and for her pedigree horses and cattle. Part of the property was immediately taken over by the Stanford Battle School together with eight thousand acres from Lord Walsingham's adjoining estate of Merton. The confiscation of the land was followed by something worse. British troops took possession of the Hall and ruthlessly devastated both house and land. Everywhere the soldiers went they left a trail of destruction; they cut down trees, oaks, pines, fruit trees, even pear trees in full blossom; they did not leave one gate upon its hinges. Mrs Rich died, heart-broken, so her surviving tenants and dependants report, at the fearful damage inflicted on her home and property. The Hall, ruined beyond all possibility of repair, was first bought by Imperial Chemical Industries, with a view to turning it into a factory, and then pulled down. Two Norwich business men, Mr A. Spruce and Mr. R. J. Seaman, purchased the two thousand three hundred acres of the estate which had not been acquired by the War Department and they put Mrs Rich's manager, Walter Brown, in charge. He is the hero of the Wretham enterprise.

Mr Brown officiates from a tiny one-roomed building which stands between the walls of the kitchen garden and the graveyard of the long since ruined church; all round are the signs and relics of war: concrete emplacements, chalked-up notices and doorless, windowless huts of rusting corrugated iron. The sense of desolation is heightened by the sight of army trucks and lorries which have been converted for the use of farm labourers. There is everywhere, despite indications of tremendous farming operations, a curious feeling that this is a no-man's-land, an owl-and-bat-haunted place marked by broken fences, crumbling latrines, tank-churned lanes and the savagely mutilated remains of avenues and copses. In the absence of the mansion house, the natural heart and pivot of a great estate, Wretham resembles a refugee settlement, an exposed, makeshift encampment.

This sad remnant has nevertheless become a profitable farm where crops have been encouraged to grow on the poor soil, once considered to be unalterably barren, as luxuriantly as at Elveden. The land round the meres has all been tilled; there are three hundred acres of barley, two hundred of lucerne, one hundred and fifty acres of peas, one hundred of splendid carrots and one hundred of sugar beet. The extensive market gardens and orchards consist of eighteen acres of blackcurrants, fifteen acres of asparagus, twelve acres of pears, seven acres of gooseberries, one hundred and thirty acres of garden peas and forty-five acres of Cox's Oranges. Twice a week a lorry travels to London with Wretham vegetables and fruit. Nearly eight hundred Essex pigs are kept on the estate, fed on sugar-beet tops; and the farm boasts one hundred and fifty Friesian cross-bred cattle.

The soil at Wretham is light, but it has never been so hostile to cultivation as the sandy heaths of the Shadwell Estate, an estate, however, which to the eye presents a far more smiling picture than Wretham. Where the one lies desolated about the foundations of its vanished hall, the other seems to exist chiefly as an ornamental setting for the great house it embraces. There is no hint of the desert in the luxuriant belts of trees and well-kept flint walls that divide Shadwell from the Kilverstone and Thetford roads; pretty flint lodges and massive gates flanked by heraldic monsters yield vistas here and there of grass-lined tracks leading away across rolling parkland and losing themselves in spinneys and copses; pheasants scream and run at any sign of a stir in the road, and a break in the trees reveals a score of more of these vivid creatures feeding in a rough field; pigeons, white, grey, iridescent and marbled fly up in front of the stranger; he is conscious of a feeling of expectancy which is entirely satisfied when he catches his first sight of Shadwell Court, looking towards it across the winding thread of the River Thet and a reed-fringed lake. The light flashes on the windows of a towered and turreted pile, a gigantic nineteenth-century folly combination of French Renaissance, Tudor and medieval motives, all carried out in flint shining like silver. The pleasure of seeing a mansion of this size inhabited and prosperous, the centre of a picturesque, carefully tended estate is so great that not a single curious thought arises. It is enough for the moment to relax in the comforting delusion that at Shadwell the re-volutionary course of the past fifty years has wrought no change.

In reality Shadwell has survived only because its owner, the late Mr John Musker, was able to adapt himself to new condi-tions. He acquired the estate as a shooting manor where scarcely any crops were grown; and his intention was to enjoy the excellent shooting. But at the same time he cherished his Breckland estate, building many stout cottages with walls of traditional flint and roofs of Norfolk reeds; he also laid out stud farms and constructed new roads. In 1939 he decided to make an attempt to reclaim the heaths and brecks of Shadwell, to farm sandy wastes where never a blade of corn had flouri-shed. An experienced manager was appointed and in that first year hundreds of acres of heather, bracken and barren sand were broken up. Barley, lucerne, sugar beet, cocksfoot and carrots were grown and a profit of four thousand pounds was made. Mustard, oats, mangolds, turnips and swedes were next grown, the mustard to be ploughed in after the summer fallow. Today every available acre at Shadwell is being farmed.

The estate is noted for its magnificent cattle; there are two hundred and forty Ayrshire and one hundred and two Red Polls. Shadwell Sultan, a handsome young bull, won first prize at the Royal Show in 1949 and was purchased by the King. And the Shadwell stud of thoroughbred racing stock is one of the finest in the world. Rows of thatched loose-boxes and stables, some of them like Staffordshire pottery cottages, add a touch of the picturesque to tracks and drives all over the estate. Shadwell is the home of a Derby winner, Bois Roussel.

Five hundred head of poultry, Old English Dorkings and Sussex, are kept at Shadwell. The birds are of extraordinary size and win prizes year after year at the dairy and poultry shows. It is a point of special interest that no extra food whatsoever is bought for them; they are free to roam where they will and to feed on what they find on the brecks.

The success of the owner of Shadwell is perhaps best illustrated by a comparison of Shadwell yields with those of the county of Norfolk as a whole, as published by the Ministry of Agriculture. In the years 1948 and 1949 the desert sand of Shadwell produced more barley and more oats per acre than the fertile territory beyond Breckland and almost equalled the rest of Norfolk in the production of rye and mangolds.

Shadwell adjoins Snarehill, which also belongs to the Musker family, and from Snarehill Kilverstone Hall can be seen standing high against a long line of trees. This house is again the centre of a thriving estate, the heart of a scene which again has undergone surprising transformation. Hall, church and village make a composition of pastoral beauty. Four gabled cottages adorn a green in the middle of which a great maple shades a silent fountain in the Italian style. This fountain was erected as a memorial by the owner of Kilverstone to the villagers who fell in the First World War and they are also commemorated by a wood called Armageddon, on the fringe of which rises a stone inscribed with hexameters composed by Lord Fisher:

Advena siste pedem reverens. Certamine caes;
Nauta audax miles celbrentur. Silva perenni
Stet monumentum illis memorique in caecula signo.

From the green a grassy path leads to the tiny, round-towered church. It has a fine Norman doorway with roughly carved pillars and capitals, but the rest of the building has been heavily restored. A gate from the flowery churchyard leads into the grounds of the Hall, almost hidden by trees and climbing roses; and church and Hall look over sweet-smelling hayfields towards the rushy, low-lying Thet and quivering willows. Countless swifts hover in translucent clouds above the scene, then suddenly swoop down arrow-straight, screaming and chasing one another, only to soar up and up again until they are the merest specks in the golden evening sky. Not even the modern lychgate with its dormer windows, shingled roof, cornice of vines and carved squirrels, not even the modern Hall which replaces an eighteenth-century flint house with a jumble of features copied from mansions in Dorset and Northamptonshire, can disturb the sense of perfect tranquillity engendered by this spot.

The portrait of Admiral Fisher by Herkomer hangs in the dining-room at Kilverstone and it is the famous admiral's son, the present Lord Fisher, who has been responsible not only for the regrettable rebuilding of the Hall but for the almost miraculous conversion of barren, derelict land, treeless brecks and stony heaths into a flourishing farm. He planted half a million trees and now farms five hundred acres, including eighty of asparagus and forty-five of blackcurrants, the best blackcurrants in Britain. They are Lord Fisher's great pride, for he is the pioneer of blackcurrants in West Norfolk. The fruit is all sent to the North of England, where colliers' wives make it into the jam that is known to clear the coal-miners' throats of dust. Lord Fisher's Folly currants have twice been awarded the Norfolk Fruit-growers' Championship Cup. His interest in asparagus was first aroused twenty-five years ago by the sight of a bush growing wild on the brecks near Thetford. He decided to cultivate it and was so successful that in a short time his original three acres had expanded to eighty and provided Thetford pickers with some eighteen hundred pounds a year. Ninety milking cows, British Friesians, are kept by a tenant farmer, and two hundred pigs, whose manure is essential for the growing of the blackcurrants, are snugly housed on Folly Farm in sties built of railway sleepers. Unlike Lord Iveagh, the owner of Kilverstone does not use or approve of combines; he considers them wasteful and believes that the necessary drying kills the germ of barley and wheat, whereas if the corn is left in the stack the germ matures evenly.

The situation of Euston in its shallow, sunny, well-watered valley flanked by noble sweeps of heathland is so bewitchingly pastoral to the eye that it scarcely seems that it could propound the problems with which the owners of Elveden, Kilverstone, Wretham and Shadwell have had to contend. Yet, except in the immediate vicinity of the Little Ouse, the soil is as poor and light as any in Breckland. Some little time before the outbreak of the last war the 8th Duke of Grafton, weighed down by death duties, decided to cultivate his Euston estate. He first ploughed up five acres of gorseland and successfully grew a crop of kale on which he folded a flock of four hundred ewes for six weeks. The land was then ploughed by tractor and sown with barley. It yielded more than ten sacks an acre though the soil was almost pure sand. During the first winter of the war the Duke reclaimed a hundred and twenty acres of heath, densely overgrown with gorse, and six hundred acres of bracken, the monstrous Breckland bracken that grows higher than a man. Mr J. Wentworth Day has described how this was done in his *Farming Adventure*:

"The bracken was first rolled, then ploughed straight into the ground, using an old International tractor, pulling a specially-made single-furrow plough a foot deep. The first crop was oats and rye. Practically no bracken was cut with the first harvest. Another thirty acres was put down to roots, seeds, kale and white turnips. All were good crops, and all were fed off by sheep.

The root land was then ploughed shallow following the sheep, while the cornland was again ploughed a foot deep and sowed with barley.

In both cases the land was then smothered with a new growth of bracken. So sixty East End schoolboys, some of one hundred and forty who were staying at the Hall, hand-picked it in the evenings. They picked it four times during the summer. In spite of this the bracken grew so fast that when the barley was eighteen inches high they had to stop picking, as the bracken was ahead of the barely. When the crop was cut it was completely smothered by bracken. Yet the yield was eight sacks an acre of good malting barley!

The Duke believes that the bracken germinates again from blackened roots, apparently quite rotten, and that it will take three, possibly five, years to get it out of the soil. Deep ploughing and potash is the secret. He intends to lay all this land down to lucerne four years after the first ploughing, keep it down to lucerne for five years, put it down to two corn crops, and then continue with lucerne again."

Until five years ago, Sparrow Hall Farm, in one of the remotest parts of the Euston heaths, had lain derelict for close on forty years. Only one crumbling flint wall of the farmhouse was left standing and the outhouses showed rent, jagged and broken above a scarlet carpet of poppies. Now every acre has been cultivated and the farm yields crops of kale, sugar beet, swedes, wheat, rye, oats and barley. Grange Farm, where the soil is pure sand, has been made to yield reasonably good crops and a wild spot known as Bayton Grove, where pines and ling once encircled a tiny mere, has been transformed into corn-fields and grazing land for sixty blue-grey Galloway cows. In each case the light soil has been ploughed as deep as from twelve to fourteen inches and the land is systematically and heavily manured.

To an age such as our own, when men are reduced to apathy by the insidious effects of nihilism, when they are stalked by horrors such as have never before been known, foremost among them not so much the fear of a violent death as the certain consequences of a world food shortage, the achievement of the great Breckland landowners brings comfort and inspiration. As a work of reclamation and organisation it equals in importance the agricultural revolution instigated by Thomas Coke in the eighteenth century. Considered against its twentieth-century background the transformation wrought in Breckland must appear even more astonishing, just as against that background Lord Iveagh and his neighbours emerge as figures more remarkable even than Coke. The owner of Holkham was one among the many exceptionally talented, energetic personalities produced by a generation which looked to the individual and not to the State for improvement and guidance. The men whose courage and enthusiasm have brought about this miracle of fertility in Breckland have been compelled to act in defiance of an age which seeks to replace individual enterprise by State control.

CHAPTER IV

WATER

I. THE MERES

THE flint and sand of Breckland enhance by contrast the attractions of the rare third element of the district, water. The banks of the few streams seem more richly green and pastoral than any park and meadow of more fertile lands, while the mysterious, haunting atmosphere of the meres is intensified by their setting of wild, sandy heath and bending pine. There are at least nine meres in Breckland, but many of them at the present time are not accessible as they lie in territory which has been given over to the War Department. The four meres in West Wretham Park, West Mere, Hill Mere, Rush Mere and Mickle Mere are of special interest, for it was here in 1851 and 1856 that the remains of Neolithic pile-dwellings were found. There were traces of a flint wall and the fragments of a rude ladder in the oozy bed of West Mere, together with deer antlers, ox bones and a great number of worked flints, whilst Mickle Mere disclosed shaped and pointed oak piles. The bed of this mere seems to be composed almost entirely of flints, some of them as large as boulders. The four most important meres may still be visited and at certain times, when no sounds but those of nature disturb the brooding hush of the heathlands, all their secret delights may yet be savoured. But military exercises frequently impair the beauty of Langmere and even, as we have seen, of Fowlmere and the Devil's Punchbowl. And Ringmere lies too close to the road from Thetford to Hockham to be left long in peace by army lorries.

Yet this mere makes a vivid impression under whatever conditions it is seen. It is situated high in a vast expanse of open heath. The hedgeless road curves slightly, commanding wide views over endless stretches of purple and brown glittering with strewn flints. The mere is almost circular with steep, ridged, grassy sides, sloping so regularly that the cavity seems at first sight to be an ancient amphitheatre, fit in its desolate setting for the performance of one of Aechylus' stark tragedies. It was indeed the scene of a tragedy which has charged the air of the surrounding heaths with a sense of doom. One of the most terrible battles between Dane and Saxon was fought close by Ringmere. The Danes landed at Ipswich in 1010 and on Easter Day they encountered Ulfkytel's forces which were encamped by the mere. Thurkytel, the son of a Dane employed as a serving man in the Saxon ranks, played the traitor, and the Danes won the day and put the Saxons to flight. The Norse scald, Ottar, thus described the battle:

> From Hringmar field
> The chime of war,
> Sword striking shield
> Rings from afar;
> The living fly,
> The dead piled high
> The moor enrich;
> Red runs the ditch.

In the *Heimskringla* the victory at Ringmere is attributed to Olaf Haraldsson, afterwards St Olaf, although he did not actually set foot in England until 1014. The saga of Sigvald includes the following lines:

> To Ulfkytel's land came Olaf bold
> A seventh sword-thing he would hold;
> The race of Ella filled the plain,
> Few of them slept at home again;
> Hringmara Heath
> Was a bed of death;
> Haarfager's heir
> Delt slaughter there.

Some of the leaders who were slain in the conflict are named in the *Anglo-Saxon Chronicle*: "Aethelstan, the King's son-in-law, and Oswig and his son, and Wulfric, Leofric's son, and Eadwig, Aelfric's brother, and many other good thanes and people out of number." The writer adds that the Danes established themselves at Ringmere and for three months they ravaged the country round about, penetrating into the Fens and burning Thetford and Cambridge.

About a hundred yards farther along the Hockham road, on either side of it, are two small, clear ponds and on several occasions I have been almost deafened by the eerie, laughing cry of black-headed gulls wheeling about the water. They breed sporadically here and at Scoulton Mere on the confines of Breckland. Their first clutches of eggs are usually collected and are sold as plovers' eggs, more than ten thousand being taken in a single spring.

From these ponds to Langmere along the Drove is less than half a mile. This extraordinarily impressive sheet of water, oval in shape with a pine-crowned knoll jutting out into its midst, unfortunately lies in an area where mock warfare seldom ceases. The mere has been encompassed with wooden palings, there are army huts and army lorries beneath the gaunt, mournful pines on the edge and tanks churn up the sand all around. Once Langmere was so solitary that to come upon it was like making a new, magic discovery. It did not seem that anyone could ever before have known the joy of emerging from the black Croxton plantations to see the starved, stony breck so unexpectedly, so mercifully interrupted by such a stretch of unruffled water. No eyes but those of curlew, gull or peewit, it seemed, could know this secret place. Ducks were scattered about the surface of the mere and on the sharp, sandy shelves of the eastern side there lay at least a score of wild swans. The swans are there still, the scream of gull and wail of peewit are as typical of Langmere today as they then were, but the uplifting sensation of perfect solitude and the unexpected has departed.

Fowlmere, although it lies close to a tank route, retains all its original character. It is the largest of the heathland meres and the most pastoral in character. And although Fowlmere is renowned for the abundance of waterbirds which may be seen disporting themselves on its wide surface, I associate it with a party of bluetits I saw there several years ago. It was a bright, windy day in early spring and dark red catkins hung and swayed from bushes whose roots and lower boughs were submerged by the water. As I stood looking at the mere, expectant yet quite unprepared for what actually happened, the tits came drifting along in their abrupt, casual fashion. The bushes were sheltered from the keen wind and there the birds paused for many minutes, some of them close to the water, others making darting, flickering movements to and fro. The enchanting combination of the richly hued catkins and pale, delicate little bodies would for one breathtaking moment perfectly repeat itself in the mere and the next instant the image would be shattered by a brilliant shaft of sunshine and a puff of wind crinkling the water.

The special interest of Fowlmere to ornithologists is, however, the fact that seven species of duck breed there, the mallard, gadwall, teal, shoveler, garganey, pochard and tufted duck. W. G. Clarke saw and watched them all, but that was the reward of many years of intimate acquaintance with the meres. The garganey, which rarely breeds so far south anywhere but in Norfolk, is, except for the mallard, the most common visitor to Fowlmere. At midday he roosts on the water, looking, with his exquisitely subdued colouring and the strange, crescent-shaped streak of white above his eye, like a duck in a Chinese painting. If some unaccustomed sound disturbs his siesta, he starts up with a flash of his pale breast; but he is a robust creature, not easily alarmed, and after a moment he settles cheerfully in the same spot again. The pochard, a marine bird, is more seldom seen, but one glimpse is enough to stamp his image on the memory. I learnt from a bird watcher at Swaffham the name of the fine creature I had noticed on Fowlmere one spring day. He had a striking glossy chestnut head and a long, pale body and his movements, swimming and diving were so swift and strong that all the ducks looked like the veriest amateurs beside him. The dark silhouette of the tufted duck, pierced by his curiously expressionless, light eye, sometimes glides across the water. Once on an April night at Croxton I heard an unusually loud, rhythmic whirr of wings overhead and was told next morning that it was a great flock of tufted duck making for the north.

The dabchick loves the dense reeds of Fowlmere's eastern margin and it is a not uncommon pleasure to find a nest with five or six white eggs in it lightly tethered to the rushes. It is an enjoyable experience to watch family parties of these amusing birds when the young ones are beginning to take to the water. Imagine a summer afternoon when the water mirrors high-piled, snowy clouds, when the reeds sigh and sway in a warm breeze and the scent of pines drifts down from the green slope above the mere. Heath birds wail and whistle, but their desolate cries, like their wild habitat, do but intensify the green pleasures of the water and the comfortable sounds of the waterfowl, the low quacking of duck saying over and over again, "I'm afloat, I'm afloat," the hoarse croak of the garganey, the clear coo of the coot and the gentle chirrup of the dabchick. The young birds move jerkily on the rushy fringe of the water, while the old ones suddenly dive and disappear for ten or fifteen seconds. When they reappear, holding in their bills some succulent morsel, the young ones scurry towards it in a most comical fashion. Sometimes they are for several seconds unaware that the parent has come up and the old bird does nothing to attract their attention. Then one little dabchick turns and catches sight of the tit-bit and in a flash they are all after it. Some take it from the parent's bill, others squabble over a delicacy dropped in front of them. The old birds are said to teach their young to dive by taking them under their wings, but the parents make no attempt on this occasion to instruct their little brown chicks in the art; and in their strenuous efforts to feed the hungry creatures they are themselves never above water for more than a minute or two.

Once as a child I was taken to see a decoy at Stanford Water, a partly artificial lake created during the mid-nineteenth century from Stanford Mere. It was March and the vast opaque-looking sheet of water was the colour of turquoise set among emerald reeds. The outer part of the strange bird-trap rose from a creek at the north end, a series of circular arches made of pliant branches and covered with folds of fine network. Gradually diminishing in size, the arches followed the winding creek to its end. On the bank a wooden paling had been built round the arches high enough to hide a man kneeling behind it from the view of the birds on the mere. At intervals here and there a hole had been broken in the paling just large enough to allow of the passage through it of a dog. In parts of Suffolk I have seen tame duck used as decoys, but on this occasion Mr Massingham, the fowler, was helped only by a small black terrier.

Mr Massingham crouched with us behind the paling and let us peep through one of the dog holes at the smooth water and the wild fowl placidly dressing their features as they floated. The dog sat quietly beside us.

"Trim!" whispered the fowler, and instantly the terrier stepped sedately through the hole on to the shelving bank of the lake. First one duck, then another, then several all together noticed the animal. He stood quite motionless and soon became an object of overmastering curiosity to the birds. The more daring of them began to swim slowly towards the extraordinary four-footed creature. By twos and threes the rest of the fowl followed the leaders. But there was nothing rash about their advance. When still at a safe distance they came to a sudden halt and, poised on the water, regarded the black shape upon the bank.

"Trim!" said Mr Massingham once more. The terrier turned and drew back through the hole. The wildfowl still stared at the spot where he had stood. A minute later he had trotted farther inward to the next hole and was showing himself once more to the ducks.

The second appearance of the terrier provoked a second fit of curiosity among the duck. With scarcely a moment's hesitation and with one accord this time, they swam forward to get another and nearer view of the dog; then again they stopped, still at a safe distance but already beneath the outermost arch of the decoy. Again the dog vanished and the puzzled duck waited. A few minutes passed and Trim appeared to them for the third time through a hole pierced still farther inland up the creek. Once more irresistible curiosity urged the birds onwards beneath the fatal arches. The game was repeated a fourth, a fifth time and the dog had lured the duck into the inner recesses of the decoy. There he showed himself yet once more. The duck advanced with caution, they paused to consider further; but they were lost. The fowler pulled a string. The weighted network fell vertically into the water and closed the decoy. There by dozens and dozens were the wildfowl, caught by means of a little dog and their own curiosity. In a few hours, we were told, they would all be on their way to the London market.

The decoy in Mickle Mere, which lies in the army-mutilated estate of Wretham, was put into working order again a year or two ago. The estate agent took six hundred duck in a season, the record takings for one day being thirty-five duck. He makes no use of a decoy dog but feeds the duck into the entrance of the decoy, then frightens them from behind into the net. This decoy is one of the oldest in Norfolk and an interesting account of it is given by Joseph Whitaker in his survey of British duck decoys written in 1918. Except for the reference to the carriage and the house it might have been written today:

"Thetford was full of soldiers, and I had much difficulty in getting a carriage, but at last succeeded and drove off to Wretham decoy. The country I passed over was typical of Norfolk, moderately undulating, well wooded, with large open fields. Here and there were big pieces of bracken, with patches of heather dotted about. Lot of striking flowers were on either hand. Mulleins reared their long stems, decked with yellow flowers, bedstraws, yellow and white, pink mallows, and lots of biting stonecrop, which seems to flourish on this dry, sandy ground.

"Six miles brought us to Wretham Park, and I found Brown, the head keeper, at home, and we walked across the park to the decoy. It lies a few hundred yards from the house, a natural piece of water called 'Mickle Mere'. It is about thirty acres in extent. Formerly there were ten pipes, but only three have been used for some years. It is a perfect-looking duck pool, and Brown said that during the season there were often thousands of ducks on it of several sorts and any day there were hundreds.

"The first pipe I saw was the largest of the three, and the biggest I have ever seen. It was ninety-six yards long and twenty-five feet wide at the mouth and about sixteen feet high at the top of the arch. This size was carried up for twenty yards or more, and the hoops, which were of flat wood, were strengthened with bands of iron, and supported as far as the bend by poles up the middle of the pipe. The hoops were fixed in strong oaken posts which came up above the bank. The netting was of wire. I have never seen these centre-supports used in a pipe before. The other two pipes were sixty-five yards long and not nearly so wide or high. The screens are of reeds six foot six inches high, the dog-jumps wood, and not high.

"The best season Brown has had he got just over 1,800 ducks. The park is well wooded, and the house, a new one to replace the one burned a few years back, is of brick, and large in size. There are several smaller pools about, which add to the attraction for ducks. Big belts of various timber trees surround the park, and it struck me as a very fine sporting property. My thanks are due to Mr Saxton Noble for kindly giving me permission to see it."

The very existence of the meres in a district such as Breckland is strange, but they have a special quality which renders them mysterious indeed. Their waters are subject to unpredictable fluctuations. Ringmere was so full in July 1950 that it overflowed the Hockham road, while during the two succeeding summers it was bone dry. The Norwich naturalist, J. D. Salmon, reported on August 2nd, 1835, that "Ringmere Pit was very dry, only a small pool of water a few yards in length and breadth and not more than a few inches in depth", which by August 24th was quite dry. In 1882 Ringmere was a deep lake 250 yards long and 150 yards wide. From 1901 to 1903 it was again dry and was covered with a closely matted growth of nettles, thistles, persicaria and dock. The following year it was full, drying up once more in the autumn. It was dry at Christmas 1909 and overflowing during the summer of the succeeding year. Records show that the height of the water in all the meres has varied in much the same way as that of Ringmere. During a dry period in 1906 the bed of Fowlmere was ploughed and harrowed and a good crop of swedes and cabbages grown there. On another occasion corn and vetches were grown on the bed of the Devil's Punchbowl. A man living on the edge of Fowlmere in 1830 assured J. D. Salmon that when the meres were high wheat was very dear and when the water was low wheat was cheap. But in 1859 Fowlmere was dry and wheat cost £11 a ton, while in 1884 it overflowed and wheat cost £8 19s. a ton.

For long no satisfactory explanation of these curious fluctuations was forthcoming. W. G. Clarke decided that rainfall alone was responsible for the changes in the depth of the water, not as surface water, for very often ponds and wells on higher ground than the meres contained water when the meres were dry, but in so far as rainfall affected the saturation level of the chalk by which the meres were surrounded. As the saturation level rises in the chalk, so the waters of the meres increase in depth, and as it falls so the waters waste until, when the saturation level is below the bed of the mere, it becomes absolutely dry. According to some geologists the meres came into being from "pipes" in the chalk, originally filled with drift sand. After heavy rains these pipes would become charged with water. As the level of saturation in the chalk rose, the waters would ascend, and gradually expand until basins were formed.

Whatever the scientific explanation of these singular changes in the aspect of the meres, the variations seemed unaccountable and fraught, therefore, with evil in the popular imagination. The waters were shunned as the haunt of the Devil. Fish and waterfowl bred there unharmed when the waters were high, and when the basins were dry neither sheep nor cow might graze upon the juicy vegetation which sprang up on the muddy slopes. Farmers who were foolhardy enough to drive their cattle on to the natural enclosure formed by the Langmere peninsula always suffered some disaster. Traditions of witch-craft persisted at Wretham until the present century and the only reliable test was considered to be that of throwing the suspected person into one of the meres. If the Devil succoured his own and she floated, her guilt was held to be established beyond doubt.

A writer in the Victorian publication *Leisure Hour* for 1887 describes how in February 1851 the son of a cottager of Croxton, employed to scare birds on the land adjoining Fowlmere, came to grief in the reed beds round the partly dried bed of the mere. Attracted by the great height of the reeds, which looked like a forest, the little boy wandered from his post of duty. No sooner had he advanced a few steps on the muddy bed of the lake than he began to sink. He called frantically for help, but there was no one to hear him. The mud slowly reached his waist and soon, he thought, it would be over his head. He stopped sinking, however, when he was covered up to his arm-pits. It was then half-past three in the afternoon. In the absolute stillness he could hear the distant trains on the Thetford–Norwich line. He shouted again and again but there was not a soul near. Evening soon closed in, followed by a night that was not only pitch dark, but cold and tempestuous. The pines, groaning

Great Cressingham Manor

The West Front, Castle Acre Priory

Tombs of the Herlings and the Lovells, East Harling

The College of St John the Evangelist, Rushford

The Little Ouse at Brandon

Eriswell

Former vicarage,
Methwold

A heath near Swaffham

Half Moon Plantation,
Thetford Chase

the day.   This do I while I may.   This did I when I myght   God help will this worlde last

Fresco in the gatehouse,
West Stow Hall

The south door, Santon
Downham Church

Cottages in Magdalen Street, Thetford

The Wesleyan Chapel, Eriswell

Oxburgh Hall

and lurching far above the poor boy, the reeds, shivering and tossing and shrilly whistling about his head, swallowed up his ever-feebler cries in their own angry protests against the wind. The boy said afterwards that he stopped calling for help but remained fully sensible the whole of the night. By morning he was powerless with cold and could no longer utter a single cry. About two hours after it was light he heard a man moving among the rushes. He had no voice to call out, he could make no sign and thought his only hope had gone. The sound died away. After half an hour of the most dreadful suspense the boy again heard someone pushing through the reeds. This time, by some miracle, the man caught sight of the child's head and shoulders emerging from the mud. It was only after a great struggle that the mere relinquished its prey. By the time the rescuer had gained the shore proper with the boy, the lad was completely paralysed with cold and unable to speak; he had been nineteen hours in the mud. The man who had saved him was from Croxton, too, and took the boy home, much to the surprise of his parents who had accepted his disappearance very philosophically and had accounted for his absence by assuming that he had gone to spend the night with his grandmother at West Wretham. A doctor from Thetford was quickly in attendance and after a week the boy was none the worse for his mishap.

As recently as ten years ago this same mere, the most poetic of Breckland's haunted waters, was the scene of a moving visitation. An airman was flying low over the glassy lake on a day of great calm when, looking down, he saw in the water the sorrowful face of a most beautiful woman, so much enlarged that it almost covered the surface of the mere. When he described his experience to his friends they ridiculed him; but soon after he was again passing over Fowlmere, this time with a companion, and they both saw the lovely features in the lake below them. Greatly stirred and anxious to solve the mystery, the two men took a boat and rowed out to the middle of the mere. They saw nothing but the brown, silent water, they heard nothing but the quacking of mallard and gadwall. But happening to glance upwards to the spot whence they had first seen the vision, there was the same enigmatical face gazing down at them from a full-bosomed cloud.

2. RIVERS AND PARKS

If an Englishman were to describe the characteristics of his native land to a foreigner who had never set foot there, it is most unlikely that he would mention Breckland. The orchards and hopfields of Kent, the Downs at lambing time, the peaceful valleys and farms painted by Constable, the dales and moors of the North, all these would at once spring to mind, but even a lover of Breckland would not dream of asserting that it was typically English. Yet it was the homely verse of Breckland's only poet, faithfully recording the scenes of his daily toil as a farmer's boy, that inspired W. H. Hudson with feeling for the English countryside long before he ever knew it. He found a copy of Robert Bloomfield's *The Farmer's Boy* in an old book-shop in Buenos Ayres and it imprinted on his mind a picture of life in remote agricultural England which still seemed to him, after he came to this country, to express the essence of the rural scene.

"I visualised the . . . entire harmonious life," he wrote, "I was with him from morn till eve, always in the same green country with the same sky, cloudy or serene, above me; in the rustic village, at the small church with a thatched roof where the daws nested in the belfry, and the children played and shouted among the gravestones in the churchyard; in the woods and green and ploughed fields and the deep lanes—with him and his fellow toilers and the animals, domestic and wild, regarding their life and actions from day to day through all the vicissitudes of the year."

This description does not match the face that Breckland has so far worn in this account. Bloomfield does indeed speak of "a slope of burning sand" where shepherd boys had met to play and of the "bleak, unwooded scene" near Castle Hill, Thetford, but his subjects for the most part lay close to the slow, sedgy Little Ouse where it meandered with its nameless tributaries about Honington, Sapiston, Troston and Euston. Breckland is, after all, part of East Anglia and it cannot entirely escape the net of little rivers that run all over Norfolk and Suffolk. The Little Ouse and the Thet, the Lark, the Nar, the Wissey and innumerable streamlets vary the arid character of the district with parks, watermeadows and marshes. But nowhere in this desert of sand and flint is there a more refreshing, verdant oasis than Bloomfield's country.

The slim, leatherbound volumes of *The Farmer's Boy* and *Rural Tales, Ballads and Songs,* published in 1800 and 1802 by Vernor and Hood, Poultry, lie in front of me as I write, the first inscribed in a flowing hand in faded brown ink: "A present to Robert Fellowes from his Grace the Duke of Grafton, July 4th, 1800." Though a century and a half have passed since the obscure country boy brought fame to his native place, his poems and the richly textured pastoral wood engravings by Bewick's pupil, Nesbitt, which illustrate them, accurately reproduce the atmosphere evoked by those unspoilt parks and villages watered by the Little Ouse. The truth of the descriptions was still acknowledged by Suffolk people as recently as twenty years ago when recitations of passages from *The Farmer's Boy* were heard with the greatest pleasure at Christmas parties in the country. The poem scales no heights and the charming fidelity of the writer to his homely subjects is often marred by unsuccessful attempts to generalise in the fashionable grand manner of his day. But the verse flows on like a crystal stream and poetic feeling glows in lines like those describing Giles's morning walk in fields where pastures border on open heath:

The sporting white-throat on some twig's end
Pour'd hymns to freedom and the rising morn;
Stopt in her song perchance the starting thrush

Shook a white shower from the blackthorn bush,
Where dew drops thick as early blossoms hung
And trembled as the minstrel sweetly sung.

And the account of Giles's expedition on a winter night to find
his flock conveys something of the vastness of nature:

> With saunt'ring step he climbs the distant stile,
> Whilst all around him wears a placid smile;
> There views the white-rob'd clouds in clusters driv'n,
> And all the glorious pageantry of heav'n.
> Low, on the utmost bound'ry of the sight,
> The rising vapours catch the silver light;
> Thence Fancy measures, as they parting fly,
> Which first will throw its shadow on the eye,
> Passing the source of light; and thence away,
> Succeeded quick by brighter still than they.
> For yet above these wafted clouds are seen
> (In a remoter sky, still more serene)
> Others, detach'd in ranges through the air,
> Spotless as snow, and countless as they're fair;
> Scatter'd immensly wide from east to west,
> The beauteous 'semblance of a *Flock* at rest.

Bloomfield's picture of minute insects on a summer day vividly
recalls not only the experiences of a siesta by the side of a field
near Sapiston but the observations of Werther as he watched
the busy movements of myriads of creatures in the grass where
he had sunk to ponder on his unfortunate passion:

> Just where the parting bough's light shadows play,
> Scarce in the shade, nor in the scorching day,
> Stretched on the turf he lies, a peopled bed,
> Where swarming insects creep around his head.
> The small dusk-coloured bettle climbs with pain
> O'er the smooth plantain leaf, a spacious plain.
> Thence higher still, by countless steps convey'd,

He gains the summit of a shiv'ring blade,
And flirts his filmy wings, and looks around,
Exulting in his distance from the ground.
The tender speckled moth here dancing seen,
The vaulting grasshopper of glossy green.
And all prolific Summer's sporting train
Their little lives by various pow'rs sustain.

The poem is divided, like Thomson's *Seasons*, into four parts
and was clearly much influenced by the far greater work. But
whereas Thomson draws inspiration from different districts,
treating of nature in a general way, Bloomfield limits himself
to the country he knows best. He was born at Honington, the
son of the village tailor, in a low thatched cottage, one of a
half-ruined row in this quiet place. George Bloomfield died
when Robert was a year old and his widow, in order to maintain her six children, opened a dame's school. There is a
red-brick Victorian school on the site now, next to the churchyard, and the sing-song voices of little children repeating their
multiplication tables echo among tombstones wreathed with
pink roses and add a homely touch to the elegant church porch.
Bloomfield was himself a pupil at his mother's school, but
when he was no more than seven years old his mother married
again and, apart from two or three months' instruction in writing from a schoolmaster at Ixworth, he was from this time self-
taught. At the age of eleven he became a farmer's boy employed
by his uncle, William Austin of Sapiston. He was small and
weak and his master soon realised that Robert was unfitted for
work on the land. His brother George, therefore, who was a
shoemaker in London, found him employment in the same
trade. He plied it for nine years, married the daughter of a
Woolwich boatbuilder, and having set up house in a single
room in Bell Alley, Coleman Street, wrote *The Farmer's Boy*.
He submitted the manuscript to Capel Lofft of Troston Hall,
a mile or two from Honington, for the squire was known beyond the confines of his county as a man of taste. Capel Lofft

boomed the rustic poet to such an extent that, within three years of its publication, twenty-six copies of *The Farmer's Boy* had been sold. Bloomfield, like many artists of humble origin, achieved his reputation largely on account of the circumstances which his patron described in his preface to the poem and not in spite of them.

The small Elizabethan house inhabited by Capel Lofft still looks much as it must have done in Bloomfield's day, surrounded by the same venerable oak, elm, chestnut and ash trees which the squire named after the immortals Homer, Sophocles, Virgil and Milton. He was himself a writer who, much to Charles Lamb's disgust, made a habit of signing his undistinguished sonnets C. L. But his special pride was his discovery of Robert Bloomfield, of whom he wrote:

"I rejoice that I at length have been made personally acquainted with him: that I have seen him here and at his Mother's and at Bury: that I have discours'd with him: that we have made our rural walks together: that I have heard him read some of those Poems which are not yet printed; but which when they shall be, will support fully and extend the Fame he has acquired. Though I have spent, occasionally, much of my life among persons worthy of Admiration and of Esteem, I can recollect few days so interesting and so valuable to me as these."

The land farmed by William Austin belonged to the Duke of Grafton who, delighted with the rustic poet's descriptions of Euston, secured for him a post in the Stamp Office.

He was the 3rd Duke, the same who presented the copy of *The Farmer's Boy* to Robert Fellowes. He was Secretary of State, First Lord of the Treasury and Lord Privy Seal, though he hated to be long away from Euston. Fox visited him there and life on the estate during his time is portrayed by a young Frenchman, François de la Rochefoucauld, who with his brother, Alexandre, and a Polish companion, Maximilien de Lazowski, lived for a year at Bury St Edmunds and kept a diary of various tours he made in Norfolk and Suffolk. The house at that time was not the red-brick mansion we see today, but an imposing classical structure of stone built by Lord Arlington in the reign of Charles II, who with a lively retinue was a frequent visitor to Euston. The house was destroyed by fire in 1902. La Rochefoucauld tells us that breakfast was taken at nine o'clock, by which time the ladies were fully dressed, with their hair properly done for the day. The meal consisted of coffee, chocolate or tea and bread and butter, and as the morning newspapers were read during the collation, conversation was limited. From ten o'clock until four in the afternoon each member of the party followed his own pursuits, hunting, fishing or walking. At four o'clock the household would foregather ceremoniously in the drawing-room, where La Rochefoucauld found the standard of politeness uncomfortably high. Dinner lasted four or five hours, of which the first two were spent in eating. Toasts were drunk to Mr Pitt, Mr Fox or Lord North and conversation was free and frank. Among the guests was Lady Hervey, wife of the famous Frederic Hervey, Earl of Bristol and Bishop of Derry, who built Ickworth House. Lady Hervey was then a woman of fifty, brilliant and commanding, her husband a man of great intelligence and lively personality.

Apart from the house itself, Euston looked to La Rochefoucauld much as it appears to us today. It is hard to understand how Evelyn, on a visit there in 1671, could have considered the setting of the mansion as "dry, barren and miserably sandy". But no doubt the planting of woods and trees, in the planning of which Lord Arlington followed Evelyn's advice, did much to overcome the bleakness of the prospect and the sandstorms of which Evelyn complained. By the time Horace Walpole came to Euston in 1753 he could not help admiring "the fine old woods", though he thought the house "old and bad". The park was watered then as it is today, by a winding stream swelling here and there into a little lake or cascading over a weir; it is still crossed by the same flat bridge, commanding on one side a most romantic view of foaming water and part of the house, and on the other of a sluggish river, deep meadows and the classical outline of Euston Church.

The church is the only one in Breckland not built of native material. The square tower of golden stone and the arched and circular openings perfectly harmonise with the pastoral guise of Breckland in this spot, with the vast landscape garden stretching away behind it, where a domed and pilastered temple tops a low hill, where cattle browse in picturesque groups beneath oak, elm and spreading cedar and where white paths lead away over the delicate grass and seem to vanish into the sky. Clear, even light floods the interior of the Stuart church from the lofty windows and shows to advantage the rich carvings of pulpit and altar-piece, attributed to Grinling Gibbons. The altar-piece is a bold relief of the Last Supper set in a frame of full-blown roses, daisies and Canterbury bells, surmounted by a grieving angel which could not be by any other hand than Gibbons'; and the pulpit is covered with swags of flowers and fruit and plump cherub-heads. The buoyant, robust character of this sculpture is translated into plaster on the ceiling of a small side-chapel and into marble in a memorial to Henry Arlington. He was the last Lord Arlington, his only daughter marrying the Earl of Euston, who afterwards became the 1st Duke of Grafton.

The present hall cannot compare architecturally with the original building, but it has nevertheless an irresistible charm. All the luxury and prosperity of Edwardian England is preserved in that view towards the mansion from the bridge by the weir. It is high summer, yellow lilies star the water, the air is filled with the cry of swifts and with the delicious rush and tinkle of the falling stream. Curtains of willows sweep and billow over the river and beyond them can be glimpsed ravishing slopes and the trimmest of gardens. The large windows of the red-brick house are shaded by red and white striped awnings and on the edge of the broad walk that leads behind it tea roses trail about immense tree-stumps. It is as though time was arrested on a July day some fifty years ago.

The tiny village, close at hand, fully sustains this impression. Tiny, creeper-hung, lath-and-plaster cottages stand low on either side of a wide green, shaded by magnificent oaks, limes, beech trees and elms and, dominating the prospect at the end of the green, a gigantic cedar with twisting trunk and an impenetrable canopy of dark fronds guards the gate of Euston. This place is unconscious of the rupture between squire and tenant; the cultivated fields beyond the village may know the bright colours and the clatter of modern farm implements, but here, where the cottages cluster on the fringe of the park, the day of the flail and the sickle lingers yet, and Bloomfield's descriptions of "Euston's watered vale and sloping plains" are as faithful now as when they were written and when they were repeated round the hearth of hall and farm during the earlier years of this century.

Beyond Euston the stream is joined by another stronger branch of the Little Ouse which rises near Garboldisham, on the edge of Breckland, and, strengthened by a maze of thread-like rivulets, ripples by the great trees and emerald park of Riddlesworth, meanders through Melton Paddocks and at Rushford enters upon an exquisite scene of moist beauty and unbroken quiet. Here the more customary combination of the classical mode with Claudian vistas is replaced by a harmony of Gothic architecture and green glades enclosed by tall limes, ash trees and yews. The river flows under a medieval flint bridge, each of whose three arches is decorated with a trefoliated niche. Water-lilies float on the stream and great yellow irises embroider the banks where scattered, thatched cottages lie so deep in the clasp of ivy and the shade of mossed boughs that they look more like last year's nests than human dwellings. A muddy path runs through flowering reeds and past blossoming elders to the church, separated by a low brick wall from what appears to be a miniature college, brought by some magic to these unlikely surroundings. The simple Early English windows of the church and the great, square tower of shining flint are in striking contrast to their luxuriant setting and to the pretty late

Gothic structure confronting them. The interior of the church is disappointing, for it was thoroughly restored by Mrs Musker of the Hall in 1901. Floor, roof and screen shine with pallid varnish and unsightly stencils disfigure the walls. The irritation aroused by this exhibition of bad taste is instantly soothed, on emerging from the south door, by the view of the college, for that is indeed the nature of this adorable building, framed by the curves of the church porch. The college of St John the Evangelist was built in 1326 by Edmund Gonville, founder of Gonville Hall, Cambridge. The entrance to the building is a pretty Gothic Revival cusped arch festooned with pink roses. To the left is a tall chimney-stack ornamented with a quartre-foil in a freestone panel, while a gable on the right is pierced by a large Perpendicular window. There are no ground-floor windows. From the upper traceried lights flint walls stretch unbroken to the untrimmed grass where pheasants keep company with domestic hens. No student has set foot in the college for many a long year; it is deserted, yet the porch is freshly whitewashed, the step scrupulously swept. In this spot upon which tranquillity rests like a spell it is easy to imagine some mysterious, loving visitant from the time when young canons sat at their desks in those high windows. The discovery of the cleaner's identity hardly disturbs this impression. Passing to the right of the college, it becomes apparent that the façade seen from the church porch is but one side of what must once have been a quadrangle. Another side survives and is inhabited by cottagers, among whom a little, wrinkled old woman, the owner of the hens, tends both church and college.

After passing through Thetford the Little Ouse gains in certainty, power and rapidity, and now no more a stream, but an acknowledged river, makes a band of willows, water avens, rushes and marsh flowers across sandy warrens and belts of pine. It would seem almost impossible to follow its course on foot, so rank is the vegetation on either bank, but a choked, neglected haling path runs first, from Thetford as far as Santon Downham, on the Norfolk side of the water and then, from

Santon to Brandon, on the Suffolk side. Thistles grow there to a height of six feet and with giant prickles make vicious attacks upon the traveller's legs, nettles of prodigious size seem imbued with hateful volition, so determined are their attempts to sting the intruder's face and bare arms, hordes of insects hum threateningly about his head and alder branches reach out to fling him to the ground. But if he perseveres against these obstacles he is rewarded by the sight of a riot of colour more exotic than anything cultivation could show, by thousands of blossoms upon which no human eye but his own has rested. The purple of thickly clustered, spiky loosestrife sets off the brilliant magenta of row upon row of willowherb; meadow-sweet and meadow rue foam among the yellow stars of the flea-bane and the voluptuous cups of the burmarigold; the tender, translucent lilac of valerian and comfrey shines against the flesh-coloured blooms of the hemp agrimony. The splendour of the scene is still more enriched by the bright wings of countless butterflies fluttering about the flowers. Clouded Yellows, Painted Ladies, Red Admirals, Small Tortoiseshells, Camberwell Beauties and Peacocks bejewel the glittering texture of the banks, as many as six or seven insects sometimes sunning themselves upon the head of one plant. Dragonflies, gleaming sticks of blue-gold and carmine, tremble above the stream, a kingfisher sits motionless on a willow bough, then suddenly takes alarm and skims along the surface of the water, a streak of metallic blue-green.

At the unfamiliar sound of human footsteps on the tangled path waterhens start up from the reeds, a gadwall whirls aloft with much to-do and circles about in terror before finding its way back to safety, voles flop nervously into the river and vanish, and a heron glides upstream with strong, slow wingbeats. At Santon Downham the gigantic wheel of a derelict staunch overshadows the stream. When traffic still passed along the Little Ouse between Thetford and Brandon, as it did until recent years, navigation on the swift current was made possible by staunches serving the same purpose as locks. The

water was held up by an oak door which was raised by chains
working on an axle, at one end of which was a large wheel.
The operator trod the spokes and by turning the wheel wound
up the chain and raised the door. In the river below the staunch
was a deep pool. The "staunch hole" at Santon Downham is
still relatively clear of the weeds which everywhere encumber
the abandoned stream and it is a favourite place for fishing
and bathing.

The Little Ouse adds unexpected grace to flinty Brandon.
Behind the Ram Inn a grassy path leads to the river bank and
the view towards the town from the watermeadows is one
of the most serene and soothing in Breckland. The reflection of
the simply designed, modern bridge, faced with flints knapped
at Brandon, red roofs, the dark bulk of warehouses, the blue
foliage of immense willows and the pale, hazed sky of high
summer in the stream is like a brilliantly detailed Dutch painting. Swifts dart under the arches sipping the water and screaming as they fly, the startling seedpods of kingcups shine in the
deep, moist grass, the mingled fragrance of tansy and pepper-
mint fills the air and the current gently slaps the sides of boats
moored beside the Little Ouse Hotel, where shaven lawns and
beds of roses go down to the river's edge. It is hard to remember that this peaceful scene lies but a stone's throw from bleak
wastes and dreary plantations.

No Breckland river offers such variety and charm as the
Little Ouse and there is no other park in Breckland of such vast
extent which is more truly pastoral than Euston; but there are
other lands and other more memorable buildings than Euston
Hall which owe their character to the watery element. Among
the guests whom Rochefoucauld met at the Duke of Grafton's
table was Sir Thomas Gage of Hengrave, "one of the most
agreeable and charming people it is possible to meet. His wife
is most engaging. They belong to an ancient Catholic family
and they have recently restored their old and ugly house and
live economically."

Hengrave stands in the Lark valley whence tiny streams feed

the ornamental waters of the park. M. de la Rochefoucauld must have been curiously insensitive to speak of the house as he did, for he had earlier in his diary expressed a distaste for the classical style of Ickworth, and Hengrave was not only utterly dissimilar in manner to the Marquis of Bristol's house, but the poetry of both the building and its setting must, so one would have thought, have struck a foreigner who commented on the contrast between Swaffham's orderly, freshly painted houses and the wildness of the heath. Hengrave Hall lies close to the road, where opposite the gate pretty thatched Gothic Revival cottages stand among firs and elms. Whenever I have been there the whole place has been steeped in that magic, changing light which has always seemed so much more intense in Suffolk than anywhere else. In the deep silence which enfolds village, hall and church, the rustle of a falling leaf, the sound of one's own hesitating footsteps in the drive, seem full of portent. The smell of damp earth and river weeds assails the nostrils, wood-pigeons call from the dense trees on the right, then through a screen of arched, dwarfed limes the front of the house is seen, a silvery, pinnacled shape, so light, so unlike many of the heavy structures of the Tudor period that it might be a mirage. The colour of the brick may account for this impression, for it is white, while the mullions are of the palest stone. Suddenly against that blanched background the figure of a nun appears walking with bent head across the immaculate lawn which spreads to the foot of the house.

Hengrave is now a Catholic institution, a not unfitting end for the home of a great Catholic family. It dates from 1525 and its first owner, Sir Thomas Kytson, a London merchant, is said to have had a hand himself in designing it. From the Kytsons it passed to the Gages, after whom the greengage, first grown at Hengrave, is named. It was Sir Thomas Kytson's son who appointed the madrigalist John Wilbye Household Musician at Hengrave. He was nineteen years of age when he took up his post and he remained there until 1628, when he was fifty-four. During that time he published two sets of madrigals, which show him to have been perhaps the most inventive of all the great English madrigalists of the late sixteenth and early seventeenth centuries. He was the son of a farmer, born at Diss, and he died wealthy and unmarried, having composed nothing after his retirement from Hengrave. Wilbye occupied a special chamber in the house, marked now by a tablet, which adjoins the musicians' gallery in the Great Hall. An inventory of the furniture of the composer's room was taken in 1602. There were two curtains of green and white at the windows, a chair was covered with a green cloth, a red and blue coverlet decked the bed, there was a great cushion of tapestry, a pewter water-pot and a staff to "beate the bedd with". The collection of musical instruments at Hengrave at that time included six viols, six violins, seven recorders and four lutes as well as hautboys, sackbuts, fluts and virginals. Wilbye's compositions were performed again in the very hall where he had first tried them out by madrigal societies from Norwich in 1927 and from Cambridge in 1932.

After leaving Hengrave the Lark, always an intricate river, begins to divide, to twist and turn, to embrace the heath in numbers of moist arms; it waters the great park and replenishes the long narrow lake of Culford on one side and on the other, swollen by a spring from Wordwell, it gives West Stow the intriguing appearance of a series of rush-girt islands joined by bridges or connected by shallow fords. West Stow Hall lies between two branches of the river and fine trees shade it on every side, while the dark crowns of pine and fir immediately behind the house throw into relief its warm pink brick and the pallor of a white horse grazing in a rough field in the foreground. West Stow is now a farmhouse and considerably fallen in size and magnificence from the time when it was built on the site of a much older house by Sir John Crofts, Master of the Horse to Mary Tudor. The graceful red-roofed Tudor house is joined by a colonnade in the Italian manner to an ornate gate-house, beyond which a pink wall and ball-topped gate-piers enclose a formal garden. The whole group is dwarfed by immense black barns and outhouses. A room over the gate contains some Elizabethan wall-paintings representing a hunting scene and four of the seven ages of man surmounted by a wide frieze of Tudor roses and foliage issuing from the heads of basilisk-eyed monsters. Frieze and figures cannot be by the same hand, for the one is highly finished and accomplished, while the others, suggested by little more than outlines, have all the charm of the primitive. A huntsman carries upon his wrist a falcon larger than an eagle; he sways backwards from an incredibly tiny waist and can only just balance on minute feet, which are always seen in profile though the body confronts the spectator; an ardent lover clasps his lass with arms of prodigious length; and upon the meagre body and spindly legs of a middle-aged onlooker is set a towering neck and ruff topped by a tiny head in much too large a hat.

Upon leaving West Stow the Lark flows on eventually to join the Great Ouse below Littleport, passing close to Mildenhall and entering the Fens just beyond Barton Mills. This is a place which is still full of poetry, although high above the watermeadows hangars show their graceless silhouettes against the sky and, through a network of barbed wire, aeroplanes can be seen congregating like giant locusts in motionless glittering groups, or settling on the runways or rising up above them. But the rare aromatic field artemisia and the grape hyacinth grow near the river, where past the staunch and the Bull Hotel, an old dormer-windowed coaching house, a scene of perfect tranquillity unfolds itself. The water is crystal clear between its brilliant, shelving banks; it moves imperceptibly so that it seems a narrow lake rather than a river. Willows, hollow, gnarled and ivy-clad, and a huge chestnut make an impenetrable screen above the green margins of the stream. Aeroplanes, the heavy traffic on the main road, all are shut out and forgotten. It is silent, intimate, an angler's retreat or a boy's summer paradise.

The mills after which the village is named are still working, but the proximity of the aerodrome sadly impairs their rural character. There is, however, a mill on the Nar at Narborough where all the delights of such places are preserved, the regular thud of the turning wheel, the contrasting sound of water rushing from the dam, the memorable smell of river weeds, willows, slimy green posts, old rotting planks and ancient masonry.

The Nar is altogether an enchanting stream. The great ruins that lie on its banks, Pentney Gatehouse and Castle Acre Priory, distinguish it as one of the most romantic of rivers and it has everywhere along its lonely course through Breckland the character of a river seen in a dream. It flows through a changeless, timeless landscape, deeply rural, now rolling and wooded, now bright with gorse, now bleak and bare. Here a field of pale moon daisies glimmers beside the water, there a battlemented tower shows above the yellow foliage of an oak copse; now the scent of roses comes drifting down to the stream from the walled garden of a Tudor farmhouse with fluted chimneys like barley-sugar sticks; now a gracious park slopes down to the river, which suddenly becomes a lake in front of a white, silent house, milk-white with a ghostly reflection glimmering in the glassy green water. At Narford trout spring from the clear, swift brook and a fine classical mansion with a tower and a pedimented façade framed by pines and heavy foliage closes a long smooth vista. This house has long been the home of the Fontaines, whose coat of arms displays three trumpeting elephants. It can be seen in the nearby church where one Jeffrey Browne has lain since 1740 commemorated by these words: "A good companion and an honest friend, rare virtues in this age."

The house was built in the early eighteenth century by Sir Andrew Fontaine, though it was enlarged and altered in about 1860. Sir Andrew was a celebrated collector and Pope admired his taste; the poet also described him as "one of the best-bred men of his age, remarkably neat in his person". Narford Hall once housed a fine assemblage of Greek and Roman antiquities as well as important paintings, some of which the collector purchased from Houghton. Some interesting portraits still hang on the walls, Roubiliac's lively bust of Sir Andrew is still in its place and the so-called "Etty Room" is adorned with Etty's *Judgement of Paris* and *The Nymphs carrying off Hylas*, and in another nearby room the ceiling is amusingly decorated with carvings and paintings of monkeys, festoons and flowers.

But now the grounds of Narford Hall are gay with striped awnings, with flags and green and white bell-tents and marquees. This is the prelude to the annual Agricultural Show, but the scene more resembles an encampment of soldiery in some Italian Renaissance picture; for a brief moment the little Norfolk Nar becomes the Arno, Syrinx hides in the reeds and a solitary horseman riding towards the Hall is transformed into a centaur.

In the north of Breckland a promontory of dry land juts out westward into a marsh created by the Wissey and its tributaries. Here in this place, which is a natural fortress, stands a moat-encircled house which eclipses Hengrave in the intensity of its atmosphere and the richness of its associations. By the ruined church of Oxburgh, which has already been described, the road bends and, on the left-hand side, there runs an impressive crenellated wall of red brick, broken here and there by towers set on cusped corbelling. The wall is a most successful work of the Gothic Revival dating from 1835. It is at once apparent from the quality of the brickwork that it is not medieval, but this romantic interpretation of Gothic architecture is a perfect introduction to the Hall. Such a wall is fit to divide the world of everyday from the land of faery. In a few moments the house comes into view, its enchanting rosy image repeated in the dark, clear water out of which it rises. It is like a castle from one of Pol de Limbourg's illuminations, it looks as fresh as the buildings in those crisp, detailed miniatures, as untouched by both time and man, as if it had but yesterday left the bricklayer's hands. If at Euston the pleasant climate of a recently vanished order still persists, Oxburgh preserves the full flavour of days far more remote.

The house was built as a quadrangle in the manner of the Edwardian stone castles, with a tower at the entrance which dominates the whole group. The aspect of Oxburgh remains exactly the same as in the year of its erection, 1482, except that the south wing, containing a great banqueting hall, was pulled down in 1778, and that the drawbridge which originally spanned the moat has now been replaced by an arch of brick and stone. It was built at a time when fortifications were excuses for ornament rather than necessities, and to that Oxburgh owes its look of a fairy-tale castle. The tower is a work of delightful invention, displaying the extraordinary mastery to which East Anglian brickmakers and bricklayers had attained by the fifteenth century. On the north side there are massive octagons, affecting to be serious works of defence but set at naught by the treatment of the south side, where the wall is interrupted by little oriels rising up on each side of the archway and the conventional turrets are represented merely by tiny look-outs, cleverly corbelled out from the parapet tower.

Henry VII visited Oxburgh in 1487 and slept in the gateway tower. His chamber with its linenfold panelling and oaken bed contains a great treasure, a set of hangings, now used as a bed-spread, shown in an exhaustive study by Mr de Zulueta, published by the Clarendon Press, to have certainly been embroidered by Mary, Queen of Scots and her one-time custodian, Bess of Harwicke, Countess of Shrewsbury. The work consists of a variety of bird and animal devices, quaintly and endearingly named and perhaps derived from contemporary bestiaries. They include "A Feret", "A Leparde", "A Buke", "A Scolopender", "A She Dophine Fishe", a "Rhinocerote of the Seas" and a huge-billed bird called "A Byrd of America". Apple trees, roses and thistles form part of the design and one of the motives is a sleeved hand emerging from clouds to cut a vine. Across the sleeve runs a ribbon bearing the motto "Virescit Vulnere Vertus", a shield of the arms of Scotland and Mary's *impressa* as it occurs on her signet ring in the British Museum.

From whatever angle it is viewed, Oxburgh makes so satisfying a composition in its setting and is so uniform in style that it

146

continually suggests comparisons with painting, but from the park it is more like a fleeting manifestation of the spirit of the past. The fantastic array of crenellations, corbie-stepped embattlements, rich mouldings and panelling rises above coarse yellow grass and glimmers against heavy foliage. A flag hanging limply from the tower announces that a Bedingfield is in residence, as it did nearly five centuries ago when Sir Edmund, knighted at the coronation of Richard III, established himself in his new manor. A hawk poises itself overhead, a heron follows the course of the stream that flows into the moat, a pheasant cries from a far-off wood, a distant shot rings through the air. Then all signs of life fade. Only the lovely pink shape remains, a mirage flung up by Breckland's deserts.

The streams and brooks which flow into the Wissey, embracing Oxburgh with their moist arms, enrich with beds of meadowsweet and soft blue rushes all the country about Hilborough, Great and Little Cressingham, Mundford and Methwold. At Cranwich the cool-coloured reeds contrast with high fields of red poppies and yellow mustard, at Mundford they relieve the sombre background of the State forest. At Methwold Breckland succumbs almost entirely to the influence of the watery element and sand and flint give way to the purple earth of the Fens. High above the river, high above Methwold Common, rears the church tower, so lofty that its pinnacles must be hung with red lights to warn aircraft off the stony slopes of its steeple. Inside the church is the fourteenth-century brass of Sir Adam de Clifton, a life-size figure of a knight in armour with a belt of flower medallions and a lion at his feet. In 1680 this brass was stolen by a tinker who broke it into more than a hundred fragments. They were recovered and lay in the ancient church chest until 1880, when the knight was skilfully pieced together again like a difficult jigsaw puzzle, one or two parts of which have been irretrievably lost.

Sugar-beet fields and the great structure of Wissington Sugar Factory give an air of desolation to the country beyond Methwold, which is more mournful than the atmosphere of any of

Breckland's ruins or barren wastes. This empty landscape on the border of breck and fen was the home of the famous sixteenth-century husbandman, Thomas Tusser. His house stood on the site of a twelfth-century Premonstratensian Abbey near West Dereham. A barn and parts of the abbot's lodging remain to give meaning to the name, Abbey Farm, by which the property is still known. Though Essex born, Tusser had strong connections with the land watered by the Wissey, for it was here that he wrote the first of English Georgics, one of the earliest books on farming in our language, *A hundredth good points of husbandrie*; and it was here that he wrote his own epitaph:

> Here Thomas Tusser, clad in earth, doth lie,
> Who sometime made the Points of Husbandrie;
> By him, then learn thou may'st, here learn we must
> When all is done, we sleep and turn to dust.
> And yet through Christ to heaven we hope to go,
> Who reads his books shall find his faith was so.

In 1557, when Tusser's book was published, Norfolk and Suffolk were the most prosperous counties in England, and even of this territory so close to the arid heaths the rhyming farmer could write:

> More plenty of mutton and beef,
> Corn, butter and cheese of the best,
> More wealth than anywhere (to be brief)
> More people, more handsome and prest,
> Where find ye (go search any coast)
> Than these, where enclosures are most?

Today these words are as true of the reclaimed lands in the most unpromising parts of Breckland as of the farms nourished by rivers and good soil.

CHAPTER V

WHERE FLINT, SAND AND WATER MEET

THE last scene of the Breckland panorama exhibits the little town which is in every sense the heart of the district. In Thetford and its immediate surroundings all the Breckland characteristics, flint, sand and water, meet and mingle. It seems as though all the stores of flint hidden beneath the sand could scarcely have sufficed to create such concentrated, impregnable ebony of façade, tower and wall. The flints of prehistory are preserved in the museum and the remote past overshadows Thetford in the shape of the immense, tree-crowned earthwork, Castle Hill, the most considerable mound of its kind in East Anglia. It supported a Norman Keep, but local opinion, probably erroneously, ascribes its construction to a far earlier date and shrouds its origin in obscurity. According to tradition, the Hill is said to have been formed by the Devil scraping his boot after he had made the so-called Devil's Dyke at Weeting by dragging his foot along the ground. There is also a widespread belief that when the Priory was destroyed six silver bells were taken from the church and concealed beneath Castle Hill. Still another legend relates that an entire palace is hidden inside the mound. A wealthy monarch lived on the site surrounded by priceless treasures, the loss of which he so greatly feared that when rumours of an approaching enemy reached his ears he ordered castle and riches all to be buried.

The top of the mound yields a view over a narrow lane between high flint walls to the meadow where the rivers Thet and Little Ouse, crossed by the Icknield Way, run side by side. The haling path, known as Spring Walk, can also be seen. Bright with dragonflies and fanned by the quick flight of the swift, this delicious spot offers pastoral and watery pleasures as great as those of Euston or Rushford, Brandon or Brettenham. Only a few yards from the river banks the delights of the open heath are recalled by a sandy, sparsely grown expanse sweeping up to a group of pines and the long wall and pilastered gateway of a former mansion, while farther distant the great forest of Thetford Chase darkens the horizon.

Spring Walk once led to the chalybeate waters which made Thetford a fashionable spa in the eighteenth and early nineteenth centuries. An aquatint of the spot made by the Reverend Wilkinson of Thetford in 1819, the year when the Duke of Grafton laid the foundation stone of the pump room, now known as Spring House, shows an elegant bridge of white wood spanning the Little Ouse and the Thet, with Castle Hill and St Peter's Church in the background. There are no invalids resting or promenading by the water, but men are sailing, punting and rowing. The river is crystal clear, the banks are indented with picturesque little creeks, no longer there, the flint cottages and houses clustered behind the bridge among groves of elm and willow are all roofed with thatch or red tiles and sweeping to the water's edge is the bosky garden of New Place, at that time the seat of Mrs Marsham.

The spring bubbled up in a meadow near the Paper Mills, now a manufactory of patent steel pulp ware, one of only two in Europe. When taken freshly from the basin, the water was quite transparent but it became turbid after a few hours' exposure to the open air and lost its medicinal powers. Dr Accum, author of a *Guide to the Chalybeate Spring of Thetford*, 1819, recommended that it should always be taken at the fountain head and only during the summer months, from May to September. The doses he advised varied from between half a pint to two pints daily and he strongly advocated gentle exercise between the draughts of water, either walking or riding on the newly invented velocipede or hobby-horse. Dr Bailey of Thetford cites the alarming case of one John Goulding to illustrate the dangers of indiscriminate use of the spring. This robust man, aged forty-five years, laboured under some disorder of the stomach. He came to Thetford, drank seven pints of the chalybeate water daily for three days and fell seriously ill. His face was florid, his fever high and he had scarcely described his symptoms to Dr Bailey when he collapsed senseless in a state of apoplexy. The doctor saved his life by taking two quarts of blood from the temporal artery. But Dr Bailey's case book gives many instances of remarkable cures affected by the chalybeate spring. It was astonishingly beneficial in all instances of general debility. Mr F. Willett of Holborn was relieved of a hideous cutaneous disease; Mr Mathews of Ixworth was cured of fits, severe headaches and violent dreams; and a young lady who fainted after the least exertion and trembled incessantly was rendered hardy and alert. Mrs Pond, an elderly lady of Shropham, was permanently healed of dyspepsia; Mrs Lake, who had been troubled for years with gravel, was able to attend to her business and to lead a normal life after a short course of the waters, while Thomas Jones, aged forty-five, who was feeling the results of an irregular mode of living and "a liberal use of fermented liquors", was restored to brilliant health in three months. The dropsical swellings and ulcers of servant maids, the flutterings and sicknesses of young ladies—all yielded to the magic spring; John Mills, a Norwich coachman, was cured of flatulency and Mrs — of Boughton declared that the waters had rid her of gallstones. If only sea bathing had not become the fashionable panacea for all ills later in the nineteenth century, Thetford's wonderful fountain might yet be working miracles. But now the basin is overgrown and forgotten, the sides green with long-haired weeds, and though Spring Walk is still a favourite promenade its sylvan quiet has never again been broken by the bustle of the elegant world.

This side of Thetford seems to belong especially to summer, whereas the remote, strange character of the place, as approached from the railway station, strikes the eye more forcibly in the winter months. The platform of the tiny station, white and slippery with frost, overlooks the nearby warrens and groups of pines leaning at odd angles against a fiery sky. A sandy road leads down into the town, where the narrow streets and dark, shining flint houses match the starkness of the weather. Halfway down the main street the flint reaches an unsurpassed intensity of blackness in the Gothic Revival tower of St Peter's. It is like the neck of a black swan sailing above the street on the grass of the graveyard. The church has a sweet interior, the nave lit by four pretty windows whose Perpendicular frames are set with Victorian raspberry-coloured panels bordered by twisting ribbons of yellow and deep blue adorned with coats of arms.

This is the most individual of Thetford's three churches. Though many Breckland churches contain features of charm and interest and several rank with the finest works of architecture in East Anglia, they are not on the whole, as we have seen, superb masterpieces of art. This is as true of Thetford as of the surrounding country. St Cuthbert's is almost entirely Victorian, rebuilt after the collapse of its tower in 1851 without a touch of fantasy or extravagance, while St Mary's, much restored, arouses far less enthusiasm than the wild tangle of its graveyard. There is a rent in one of the churchyard walls and the jagged opening gives access to St Mary's Row. This lane of low cottages, presenting an unbroken façade of flint topped by dusky red tiles, is one of the eeriest, most foreign-looking places in Breckland.

Separated from St Peter's by a crossroad, a complete contrast to the church, is a medieval wattle and daub house, the Bell Inn, once a famous coaching inn and the subject of a painting by Morland. One of the upper rooms contains a fine stone hearth with a floral decoration painted on the wall above it, a design of dark green leaves and rosettes on a pink ground with a frieze which bears traces of lettering. A shape like a huge masculine leg stands out against the flowery background and may be part of a figure composition which was cut off by the modern ceiling.

Opposite church and inn, Minstergate Street slopes gently

towards the remains of Thetford Priory. On the way to the Priory an enamelled advertisement above a humble tea-shop recalls the period of tatting, bustles, squires and horkeys. The bright blue and white plaque illustrates the pleasures of Fry's chocolate with five heads of the same small boy whose face registers stages of emotion varying from desperation, when Fry's seems remote, to realisation, when his delighted palate assures him of the superior make of the sweet he tastes. The juxtaposition of this old-fashioned advertisement to a modern announcement of Bev, "the essence of coffee and chicory", is paralleled by the proximity of the quaint little shop to a factory where, with deafening clangs and bangs and the blaring accompaniment of "music while you work", tin boxes are made by the hundred. Almost immediately beyond the factory the Priory walls enclose a vastly different venerable world of quiet and melancholy.

It is difficult, despite plans and guides, to reconstruct the appearance of the original buildings. All that can be said of them is that they must have been of vast extent. The remains are formless masses of rough flints which look as though they had been buffeted not only by wind and weather but by fierce tides as well. Only the Priory gatehouse, a fifteenth-century structure with twin turrets charmingly decorated with flushwork, has withstood the onslaught of decay, and among the amorphous shapes of the ruins one crumbling fragment of a lofty arch still testifies to the architect's skill. It is a deep lilac colour in the failing light of a winter afternoon. Behind it, in a landscape of heath, pine and river, another medieval flint ruin and an ecclesiastical-looking building, the remains of the Benedictine Nunnery of St George, emphasise the theme of decay.

The Cluniac Priory of St Mary was once one of the greatest monastic houses of East Anglia, with possessions scattered throughout Norfolk and Suffolk, Cambridgeshire and Essex. It was founded in 1103–4 by Roger Bigod of Bungay Castle. The original Priory was in the heart of Thetford, attached to St Mary's Church, which was the cathedral of the diocese from

1070 until 1094, when the see was transferred to Norwich. The foundation stones of the buildings on the present site were laid by Bigod and the Prior on September 1st, 1107. A new church, the ruins of which form the principal part of the remains now visible, was completed by 1114, but the building of the rest of the Priory continued throughout the twelfth century. A Lady Chapel of considerable size was added to the church in the early thirteenth century as a result of miraculous events which were recorded by one of the monks, John Brame.

A Thetford craftsman who was suffering from an incurable disease prayed incessantly to Our Lady for the restoration of his health. One night she herself appeared to the sick man in a dream and commanded him to tell the Prior to build her a chapel on the north side of the church. Three times she manifested herself to the man, who then felt compelled to repeat his dream to the Prior. The Prior was impressed and ordered a wooden chapel to be made. The craftsman protested that Our Lady had wished the chapel to be built of stone, but the Prior was not sufficiently impressed to permit such extravagance. Our Lady then appeared to a Thetford woman and bade her instruct a certain monk to urge upon the Prior the necessity for a stone chapel. She ignored the vision and not long after lost the use of her arm. She then went in tears to the monk, who brought the news to the Prior. The story convinced him and the stone chapel was forthwith erected. An image of Our Lady, which had formerly stood in Thetford Cathedral, was cleaned, redecorated and set up over the altar of the new building. In the course of the work the head of the statue was found to be hollow and full of holy relics. These conferred upon the image strange powers of healing. Among the first to benefit from them were the craftsman and the Thetford woman. The news spread about the countryside and pilgrims flocked to Thetford.

The cult brought great riches to the Priory and before the end of the thirteenth century the entire east end of the church was rebuilt on a more elaborated scale. Repairs and alterations went on continuously during the fourteenth, fifteenth and early sixteenth centuries. At the time of the suppression of the monasteries Henry Howard, Duke of Norfolk, whose family and title had always been closely connected with the Priory, and whose ancestors were buried there, petitioned the King to convert it into a college for secular canons. The petition failed, however, and on February 16th, 1540, the last Prior and sixteen monks surrendered the Priory to the King's commissioners.

Three registers survive of the expenses of the Priory, dating from the end of the fifteenth century, and these give a far more vivid picture of the life of the monastery than any outline of its history could do. They reflect activities as varied as the "skeryng of rooks" from crops to preparations for royal visits and the enjoyment of entertainments provided for the monks and their guests by minstrels and strolling players. There was a royal visit in 1498 and the sequel appears among the list of payments made by Prior Roger under the heading *Necessaria*: "per manus Roberti Whall to the beer-brewer for pewter loste whan the kyng was presente—VIs." Could the pewter have been appropriated by a member of the royal retinue?

The prices of food on the occasion of this visit are interesting. They include:

Johanni Smyth pro Oleo pro coquina	XIs,	IXd.
Pro III Salmon		XVIIId.
Pro Roberto Russell pro pykerellis et anguillis	IIIIs.	
Pro halfe a syde of befe	IIIs.	
III libris dats		XIId.

Roberto Russell seems to have been a versatile man for farther on in the register he is mentioned as having received 16s. 8d. for digging foundations. This entry occurs among many references to different types of workers. Three men sang at Christmas 1506 for one shilling and the "Duchess of Norfolch's menstrell" was paid eightpence for his services on the same occasion. Robert Love received eight shillings for dyeing forty-eight yards of cloth, a Thetford maker of musical instruments repaired the "pryncs trompetts" for one shilling, the "Plomere werkyng 1 day" earned four shillings and eightpence, Richard Graner made a "new board for the hospia" for two shillings and fourpence, Thomas Aldrych designed and made the "Windowe at the heye Awteer" for two pounds eleven shillings and twopence and Edmund Drayton delivered four cartloads of flints for eightpence.

There were many other religious houses in Thetford besides the Cluniac Priory, of which nothing now is left but flint ruins. There was not only the Benedictine nunnery, the remains of which can be seen from the Priory grounds, but a Dominican friary flourished in the precincts of the Grammar School, a house of the Canons of the Holy Sepulchre was established on what is now the Brandon road, and John of Gaunt founded a house of Austin Friars higher up the river. A mouldering wall of this friary adds a picturesque note to Ford Place, while a broken arch and flint-encrusted fragments in the lower part of the garden of a Georgian house in Old Market Street, now a café, seem also to have formed part of the same building. A few piles of flints, reduced almost to the rough state in which they were first quarried from the warrens, are, apart from documents, all that testify to the bustling existence of these great buildings which, for more than four hundred years, dominated the lives of Thetford citizens and influenced the country for miles around. Thetford ruins of more recent date confirm the impression, conveyed everywhere by Breckland, that the original primitive character of the district will triumph eventually over all attempts to cultivate and civilise. Opposite the Melbourn Inn the arcaded cupola of the Town Hall, the white figure of Justice and a structure like a gallows rise above gaping walls and a mass of crumbling masonry, all thickly beset with elder bushes, coarse grass and nettles.

The colonnaded Town Hall, rebuilt in 1902, repays a visit, for it houses a collection of portraits of East Anglians made and presented to the people of Thetford by Prince Frederick Duleep

Singh, son of the Maharajah of Elveden. They include, among natives of Breckland, an amusing caricature of Capel Lofft, Bloomfield's patron, striding across a landscape recognisable as the surroundings of Troston; a lady of the Keppel family, painted in about 1760, and eighteenth-century portraits of members of the Crofts family of West Harling. As works of art the most interesting pictures in the collection are Gainsborough's captivating little oval of Mrs Oliver of Sudbury, an early work, probably painted before the artist left Suffolk, and an anonymous composition showing Arthur Young with his sister Elizabeth May. Two children pose stiffly in front of an Italian landscape enlivened by a parrot. The boy is dressed in blue and white with a black bonnet and holds two cherries in a wooden little hand; the girl wears white and pink and nurses a minute spaniel. Thomas Paine, Thetford's most celebrated son, is represented by no more than an engraving after a picture by Romney.

From the Guildhall and Market Place King Street leads back once more to the Bell and White Hart Street. Near the crossroads stands a mansion known as the King's House, because it was purchased for James I to use as a hunting lodge. The exterior of the building is not Jacobean but Queen Anne in character. The interior is not open to inspection as the house has now been put to some official purpose, but the gardens have been given up to the pleasure and recreation of Thetford citizens. They yet retain all the charm of a private place. There is a hothouse alongside the mansion which looks as if the mistress had but just been her rounds, snipping off dead leaves and re-arranging her favourite plants. A palm tree spreads itself in the centre and all round are pots of verbena, begonias, calceolarias, petunias, nothing rare, but a cloud of fragile, crinkly shapes ranging from palest pink to deep blood-red and purple. Built into the rounded end of the greenhouse are fragments of an ecclesiastical building, among them a carving of a Pascal lamb like the one at Santon Downham.

Turning once more into White Hart Street by the King's

House, which stands next to St Peter's, a timbered building on
the opposite side of the road attracts attention. It is called The
Ancient House. Nothing of its history is recorded except that
it dates from the fifteenth century. Like the collection of pictures in the Town Hall, it was given to the people of Thetford
by Prince Duleep Singh, and it is now a museum containing
many objects presented by the Prince. The interior of the house
is a fine example of its period. It is all of oak, dark with age, and
contains a few lofty, draughty rooms with carved friezes and
great stone hearths.

All the history and atmosphere of Breckland can be recalled
and experienced afresh in the little museum. On the ground
floor are housed relics of the district dating from the Old Stone
Age to medieval times, a great number of them found by
W. G. Clarke. By far the most moving of these relics are the
flint tools, of which there are many more and far more perfect
and varied examples than those to be seen at Grime's Graves.
There are large hand-axes from the Old Stone Age, found in
gravel deposits of the valleys of the Little Ouse, the Lark and
the Wissey, small fragments of Middle Stone Age tools from
Wretham Heath and Wangford Warren and countless examples of finely worked Neolithic flints. There are Bronze Age
arrow-heads found on all the higher parts of Breckland, and
simple terracotta-coloured pottery vessels from Knettishall and
Castle Acre. Small coins of the Iron Age bear designs of long-
necked birds, hedgehogs and a long-eared creature like a rabbit
on patterned background. Red-glazed Samian ware, fragments
of bowls decorated with figures in relief of dancers and laurel
leaves bear witness to the Roman occupation of Breckland. A
Roman town may actually have stood on the site of Thetford,
but it is the museum relics of Anglo-Saxon times which recall
the imagination of the visitor from heath and river valley to
the town itself. Its history proper began in the eighth century.
Theodford (the people's ford) was the centre of fierce conflicts
between the Saxons and the Danes, who eventually established
themselves on the spot and from there entered into more or less

peaceful occupation of their settlements in East Anglia. The
Saxon pottery-kilns and the work they produced have already
been mentioned. There was also a mint at Thetford from the
reign of Edgar to that of Henry II. Casts of the coins discovered
on the site show heads of Edgar, Aethelred, Canute, Harold,
Harthacnut, Edward the Confessor, Harold II, William the
Conqueror, William II, Henry I, Stephen and Henry II. The
originals are now in the National Museum of Stockholm. To
see the Thetford coins as part of the great Swedish collection is
to taste to the full their strong local flavour. The robust, naive
quality of some of the designs, the free line of the large-eyed
heads with crimped hair, and the reverse images, often a Breckland bird or flower, are all emphasised by contrast with the
intricate, conventionalised patterns of the Scandinavian and
continental coins of the period. The exciting discovery of part
of the actual town of Saxon Thetford on the New Town Estate
has been described.

The two upper rooms of the Ancient House, over which presides the death mask of Tom Paine, are devoted to the more
recent history of Thetford and to the riches of its heaths and
meres. Among many curious and delightful relics are a white
and blue plate decorated with a large bell, which belonged to
the landlord of the Bell in 1790; a memorial mug celebrating
the centenary of Wesleyan Methodism, October 8th, 1839; an
elegantly printed first-class season ticket for 1856–7, No. 987,
issued by the Eastern Counties Railway and made out to "Mr
A. H. Fison or Mr Peachey"; a tiny, mulberry-coloured,
pointed-heeled slipper, left behind by H.R.H. the Duchess of
York, eldest daughter of Frederick William II, King of Prussia,
when she stayed in 1767 at Elveden Hall; and the arithmetic
exercise-book of Thomas Davey, a pupil at Thetford Grammar
School in 1799. The gulf which divides his age from our own
could not be more eloquently conveyed than by his exquisitely
ordered and written title page.

These objects are to be found in the room at the head of the
stairway; a larger apartment adjoining it contains an exhaustive

collection of Breckland plants, butterflies, beetles, animals and birds. If the flints below retell the enthralling story of Grime's Graves, testify to the persistent influence of prehistoric man in Breckland, recall the part played by flint in church building and in the aspect of Breckland ruins and revive the excitement of personal experience and discovery, these cases of stuffed and dried creatures and of pressed flowers bring to mind all the pleasures of heath, mere and river valley. The watervole seems to be the very animal seen that hot summer day by the Little Ouse near Santon. The Red Admirals, the Small Tortoise-shells, the Peacock butterflies belong to the same day and scene. That handsome rare Swallowtail might well be one of a number I was once fortunate enough to see near Wretham Mere, where the marsh-milk parsley, on which its larvae thrive, commonly used to grow.

It is, however, the birds, stuffed and cased, which speak most clearly of Breckland pleasures. The golden Indian pheasant is part of that winter day at Elveden; as I look at him I feel again the sharp surprise and delight occasioned by his sudden exotic appearance in the snow-covered park. What delicious summer days and nights are associated with gadwall and mallard, dab-chick, wigeon and tufted duck. As I dwell on the contrast be-tween those agile, sleek creatures and the stiff, silent effigies before me, I am startled to see a Great Grey Shrike tremble with a semblance of life; he seems to ruffle his plumage, to fix me with an eye no longer glassy and expressionless. I hold my breath in momentary alarm and then realise that the movement is caused by a pliant and inadequately fixed perch and my own footsteps on a loose board.

Some of the birds once common in Breckland are to be seen seldom or no more. The Great Buzzard, a majestic, mottled and tawny creature, has been extinct for a hundred years; the white-tailed eagle, formerly a visitor to the warrens, comes no longer. I have not heard that Montague's Harrier has been seen in the district during the last fifteen years. The Ring Plover, described as very abundant at the beginning of the nineteenth century, had greatly diminished in number in W. G. Clarke's day; at the present time it is rare to find more than a pair nesting on each heath and breck which has survived afforestation and military operations. The decrease in the numbers of stone-curlews is also noticeable. For all that, the essential Breckland is not yet a museum piece, a relic of what once was. The museum is only a reflection, a reminder of what still exists within a short distance of its walls. The wild spirit of heath and mere is yet untamed and it does not seem vain to hope that, as it has survived and defied the changes of former centuries, so it will prove superior to the barbarities of our own age. The fearsome clatter of army vehicles which now banishes sleep from the beds of Thetford citizens and threatens the lives of birds and plants will pass away; the heath will endure longer than the State forests; the stone-curlew will at last reclaim its stolen territory and breed again where dusky ranks of conifers now grow, where aerodromes and army huts now stand.

CHAPTER VI

INDEPENDENT SPIRITS

It is a September Sunday afternoon at Eriswell. The light
sparkles on the flint façade of a terrace of cottages set back from
the road behind long gardens bright with sunflowers and
Michaelmas daisies. A plastered plaque informs the passer-by
that the cottages are known as Victoria Place and were built in
1852. They were erected by the New England Company for
Propagating the Gospel in Foreign Parts. The zeal which gave
rise to this little terrace in so remote a place harmonises with the
invigorating character of its Breckland setting and expresses the
same pioneering, independent spirit as an earlier building on
the opposite side of the road, a tiny cube of jetty, dressed flints
bearing the legend *Wesley Doctrine*. The day is unusually hot
and the door of the chapel stands open. Through it can be seen
the back of a young woman with a bun of yellow hair showing
under the upturned brim of a plain felt hat and a crowd of
children, fairly filling the interior. Someone is playing the
opening bars of

> Christ, whose glory fills the skies,
> Christ the true, the only Light,
> Sun of Righteousness, arise,
> Triumph o'er the shades of night!
> Day-spring from on high, be near!
> Day-star in my heart appear.

Then thin, high-pitched voices join in, making up with
enthusiasm for lack of ear.

There are still ardent chapel-goers in Breckland, there are
still occasions like this when an overflowing hall recalls the days

at the close of the last century, movingly described by Mr Michael Home, when the inhabitants of an isolated village would walk miles over the heath to hear a new preacher, who had probably travelled far himself to expound the Gospel in this remote district. The speaker, so an old lady at Fakenham told me, was usually a man as simple and uneducated as his audience. He would express himself crudely, without restraint, taking for his theme the Popish practices of the Church or drawing such lively pictures of hell and the terrors of death and judgment that his hearers yearned for the joy of conversion which alone could save them from eternal torments. Very often the meeting would end with tears, swoonings or jubilations.

The remarkable number of chapels, congregational halls, meeting-houses and tabernacles in Breckland, as conspicuous as chapels in Welsh towns and villages, bear witness to the fervour with which Nonconformity was embraced by people disposed to independence by the harshness of their environment. Chapels for Baptists and Wesleyans greet the eye at every turn in Swaffham. At Mildenhall three different sects, the Wesleyans, the Baptists and the Calvinists, are represented, the last-named by a severely plain, flint structure with the impressive words "Jehovah Jirah" over the entrance. The many meeting-houses in Thetford include a delightful Georgian example in Earl Street with a yellow, ornamental panel above a large, clear, arched central window. No village is without a house of worship for dissenters; even a tiny place like Hockham boasts a red-brick Wesleyan hall as well as a queer, rusty little chapel of corrugated iron with a tin plate over the door displaying the words "In Memory of R. Spurgin".

When the community was more prosperous than usual, Nonconformist buildings sometimes assumed the grotesque, exotic form of follies. There is an astonishing edifice at Attleborough on the Thetford road. It is an assymetrical mass of red brick, shiny red marble and white stone, with a squat tower to the left of the entrance surmounted by ornate stone pinnacles.

The entrance takes the shape of a crenellated porch, a double-pointed arch, marble columns and lavish floral decoration in the Moorish style. Immediately above the porch is an enormous Perpendicular window. It is impossible to convey the gloom that emanates from this building; it represents all the worst aspect of dissent: hostility to art is expressed not by tolerable severity but by self-satisfied indulgence in the most tasteless extravagance.

Nonconformists were numerous in Breckland by the beginning of the seventeenth century. They denied that the reigning sovereign was head of the Church of Christ, held many prohibited meetings and suffered the fiercest persecution. The principal sects at this time were the Presbyterians, later called the Unitarians, the General Baptists and the Independents. During the following century their numbers increased to several thousands and were swollen by the establishment of Methodism. Charles Wesley preached the first Methodist sermon ever heard in Breckland in 1754 at Lakenheath. Methodists at Barnham ten years later conducted their meetings in cottages because the squire refused them a site on which to erect a chapel. He died unexpectedly of a fever and the Methodists approached the new squire.

"Is it true that you prayed for the death of my predecessor?" he asked.

"We prayed that the Lord would remove every hindrance to our having a chapel," they replied.

Afraid, no doubt, that he might also be removed, the landlord lost no time in granting his tenants a site.

Outbursts of spiritual violence rarely occur during a chapel service today, but in Breckland they still find expression. The American religious mission at Lakenheath and Mildenhall, organised by a Baptist sect, is enjoying a success which in another district might well be less spectacular. Crowds flock to prayer and hymn meetings in the open air, in parish halls and churches; and these meetings are often followed by mass conversion, tremendous excitement and rejoicing. One Saturday night in the summer of 1952 in the great church at Mildenhall, where the normal congregation had shrunk to a mere sixty, nine hundred people from the surrounding villages gathered together to pray and sing. Hundreds attended the baptism of a convert from Lakenheath in the River Lark. These modern Baptists, like their earlier predecessors, believe that only entire immersion is true baptism and that baptism should only be administered to persons old enough to make a personal profession of religion.

During the seventeenth century, when the various dissenting sects were beginning to establish themselves in Breckland, there lived at Santon Downham a minister of the Church of England who exhibited as much independence of spirit as the Nonconformists. He was John Rous, who kept a diary from 1625 to 1642 which is alike remarkable for its singular omission of personal matters and for the moderation of the writer's views at so disturbed a time. John Rous was the son of the incumbent of Weeting, was educated at Emmanuel College, Cambridge, and was appointed minister at Santon Downham on September 21st, 1623, when he was thirty-nine years old. He continued, however, to live at Weeting with his father, who was old and infirm.

Various domestic changes befell the diarist during the period of his residence at Weeting. He married, became the father of three daughters, buried his wife and took a second, who brought him a fourth daughter. But to none of these events does he refer. He mentions the baptism of a fifth daughter in 1633 and announces the death of his fourth daughter, Elizabeth, in 1639. On the death of his father, Rous did not move to Santon but to Brandon, to a building called "the ministers' house", where several of the clergy of the adjacent rural parishes lived. He made one or two journeys to London and travelled also to Genoa, but the greater part of his life was spent in Breckland, then far wilder and more exposed than it is today. From this desolate retreat he watched and commented upon the storm that darkened his age, the struggle between Royalists and Puritans.

If their uncompromising surroundings inspired Breckland Dissenters with increased ardour for the cause, they enabled John Rous to retain a standpoint as balanced as his clear even-flowing calligraphy. The diary opens at the accession of Charles I, and in these early years Rous, though inclining towards a mild form of Puritanism, staunchly upholds the existing order in Church and State. On one occasion he defends the royal policy against the subversive criticism of Mr Paine of Riddlesworth and of a neighbour, Mr Howlett. "I saw hereby," he writes, "that which I had often seen before, viz. men be disposed to speake the worst of State bisnesses and to nourish discountente, as if there were a false carriage in all these things, which if it were so what would a false hearte rather see than an insurrection? a way whereunto these men prepare."

As the agitated years pass, the diarist's attitude grows less assured, though at all times he is scrupulously fair in his judgement of events. He transcribes savage lampoons on the Duke of Buckingham, but adds a warning that "those which are in esteeme and greatest favour with princes are most subject to slander of tongues, the vulgar delighting herein, who judge of all things by events, not by discretion". Yet he views the policy of the High Church party with increasing distaste and becomes more irritated by the conduct of some of his High Church neighbours, who were the "ceremonious" type of divine described in a popular satirical rhyme which Rous transcribes, entitled "The Times' New Churchman":

A ceremonious, light-timbered scholar
With a little dam-mee peeping over his collar;
With a Cardinal's cap, broad as a cart wheele,
With a long coate and cassocke down to his heele.
See a newe Churchman of the times,
O the times', the times' newe Churchman!

His gravity rides up and downe
In a long coate or a shorte gown;
And sweares, by the halfe football on his pate,

That no man is predestinate.
See a newe Churchman of the times,
O the times', the times' newe Churchman!

His Divinity is trust up into five points,
He dops, ducks, bowes, as made all of joints;
But when his Romane nose stands full East,
He fears neither God nor beast.
See a newe Churchman of the times,
O the times', the times' newe Churchman!

During the opening years of the Long Parliament and after
the outbreak of war, Rous continues to sympathise with the
Parliamentarians, but he hopes for some eventual form of
accommodation. But by May 1643, when he made the last
entry in his diary, negotiations had completely broken down and
by April of the following year Rous was dead. It is impossible
to guess how this temperate man would have reacted to the
troubled years which lay ahead. Would he have submitted to
the abolition of the Prayer Book or would he have joined some
of his more extreme neighbours in the sufferings they endured
for their faith? Mr Garey of Beechamwell, who had annoyed
the diarist with his High Church views, expiated his "lowe
congies", by sequestration and great tribulation; he was dead
by the time of the Restoration. The Reverend James Buck of
Stradbroke, "Ceremonious Bucke", as Rous called him, was
seized and carried off to Ipswich gaol. When violence thus
penetrated the boundaries of his own aloof vantage-point how
would this unprejudiced observer have fared?

In the following century, in 1737, there was born in White
Hart Street, Thetford, the most famous of Breckland men,
Thomas Paine. It is not in the least fanciful to see a connection
between the purist's return to primitive origins and the sharp
skyline of the bare heath, between the landscape that surrounded
Paine's boyhood rambles and the stark views that fostered re-
volutions and movements whose disastrous consequences are
still unfolding themselves. He cannot be blamed. Other men

foresaw the deadly effect, on all that distinguishes man from other creatures, of setting up the ideal of equality, they spoke with as much eloquence as Paine, but their voices fell on deaf ears. Even later when those effects were already being felt, no one paid any attention to the prophetic words of men like Matthew Arnold or Heine, who saw that the day was at hand when the mob would force its way into the laurel groves of the poets, trample upon them and ruthlessly pull down the statues of the muses and the busts of artists. It was useless to resist change, the seeds of which had long since been sown by other errors, and Paine was the instrument chosen by fate to hasten that change.

The story of his career is too well known to be retold here. Few men can have seen their words work upon their readers with such electrical effect. In 1775, a few months after Thomas Paine landed in America, having failed in his own country as staymaker, schoolmaster and excise officer, he published a pamphlet entitled *Common Sense*, of which 120,000 copies were sold in less than three months, and which wrought up the colonials to such a high temper that separation from the Mother Country was inevitable. During the war that followed, Paine's *Crises* put heart into the Americans when their cause seemed hopeless, nerved the country dwellers to put every obstacle in the path of the invaders and repeatedly sent up the rate of recruitment. It was in the second *Crisis*, dated January 13th, 1777, that the title appeared for the first time which has achieved all the renown its author prophesied. Paine wrote, thus christening a nation: "The United States of America will sound as pompously in the world or in history as the Kingdom of Great Britain."

Returning via France to his native Thetford, Thomas Paine renewed his acquaintance with the lonely heaths of Breckland and wrote *The Rights of Man*. More than 50,000 copies were sold in little over a week. It is not a book which can be read with much sympathy today: we have come too close to the realisation of the drab ideals advocated by the author. Yet if we read it without enthusiasm, we must acknowledge Paine's originality. Writing more than one hundred and sixty years ago, he suggests a scheme whereby all citizens above the age of fifty should receive a pension and he says of women, urging that they should be liberated from domestic bondage: "When they are not beloved they are nothing and when they are, they are tormented. They have almost equal cause to be afraid of indifference and love. Over three-quarters of the globe Nature has placed them between contempt and misery."

The little we know of Paine as a man is not agreeable. Like most reformers who profess to love mankind, he showed small aptitude for love in his personal relations. When his landlord at Lewes, where he was an exciseman, died, Paine married his daughter for the purely practical reason that he wished to share the inheritance; the marriage was never consummated and soon afterwards Paine declared that he no longer found a wife convenient. This ardent friend of the French Revolution was so touchingly simple by nature that he was dismayed by the brutalities of the mob and, though a declared enemy of monarchy, was shocked by the execution of the French King and Queen. At the same time he was assertive, dogmatic, impetuous and unimaginative. He would not brook the slightest contradiction and was incapable of calm discussion. His opinion of himself was so inflated that he would not only say "I am the author of, I believe, one of the most useful and benevolent books ever offered to mankind", but would declare that if every book in the world were burnt except *The Rights of Man*, humanity would greatly benefit by the bonfire.

It is scarcely necessary to add that Paine was insensitive to beauty. He speaks with the utmost complacence of the "mouldering ruins of pompous palaces, magnificent monuments, lofty walls and towers of the most costly workmanship" which would be left in the wake of the champions of the "fair cause of freedom". He never alludes to the charms of nature.

He was braced, like the Nonconformists, in his independence

of thought by his early Breckland environment, yet, like them, and like the Reverend John Rous, he paid no heed to it. But within a short distance of Tom Paine's house in Thetford there lived in our own century a naturalist who wrote with such intimate knowledge of the flowers, the birds and the insects, of the geology and antiquity of Breckland, that his book is still the best possible companion to the district and there can be no better end to an attempt to describe Breckland than a brief appreciation of the man to whom it owes so much and to whom I have already had occasion to refer many times. W. G. Clarke was not a native of Breckland. He was born in Yorkshire of East Anglian parents in 1877 and came to Thetford as a boy. He was educated, like Tom Paine, at the Grammar School and at the age of fourteen he was apprenticed to his father as a printer. By 1897 he had become a journalist on the staff of the *Norwich Mercury*. He later became President of the Norfolk and Norwich Naturalists' Society, Honorary Secretary of the Prehistoric Society of East Anglia and Fellow of the Geological Society. He died in 1925.

A photograph which forms the frontispiece of *In Breckland Wilds* shows a man with a gentle face and narrow, sloping shoulders wearing dark glasses and a cloth cap and standing behind the giant leaves of a gonnera. As one of his friends said, he was physically not unlike the Neolithic inhabitants of Breckland. And indeed he had some subtle instinct for finding the remains of those ancient people which may go with physical conformation, and which was developed by close acquaintance with the heaths. He picked up flints with the greatest of ease, and fine specimens found by him are to be seen in the British Museum as well as at Thetford and Norwich.

W. G. Clarke was more of a naturalist than a writer; his knowledge of botany and ornithology was so great that he could say how many varieties of wild flowers there might be on one particular stretch of heath and what species of birds and how many pairs had nested there during all the years he had known it. But though he had a mind like a card index and his book is full of lists and facts which he would never omit for the sake of style, he was a scientist with a sense of poetry. When he writes of the colours of the warrens in autumn, of the cries of curlew and lapwing, of the grace of the water-aven, his prose takes on a rhythm which inspires his reader with that passion for the wilderness which was the mainspring of his life.

His distress during the First World War at the destruction of rare flowers and the scaring of birds by the establishment of the great training camps near Thetford was acute. He has mercifully been spared the much more drastic changes which have come to Breckland during the last twenty years. His book is a portrait of a district which now only exists in a mutilated state. To cling to what remains, indeed to make that portrait once more entire, must be the aspiration of all who have felt W. G. Clarke's love of the timeless waste, who have followed his minute accounts of all the plants and creatures that grow, creep, run and lie upon the heath.

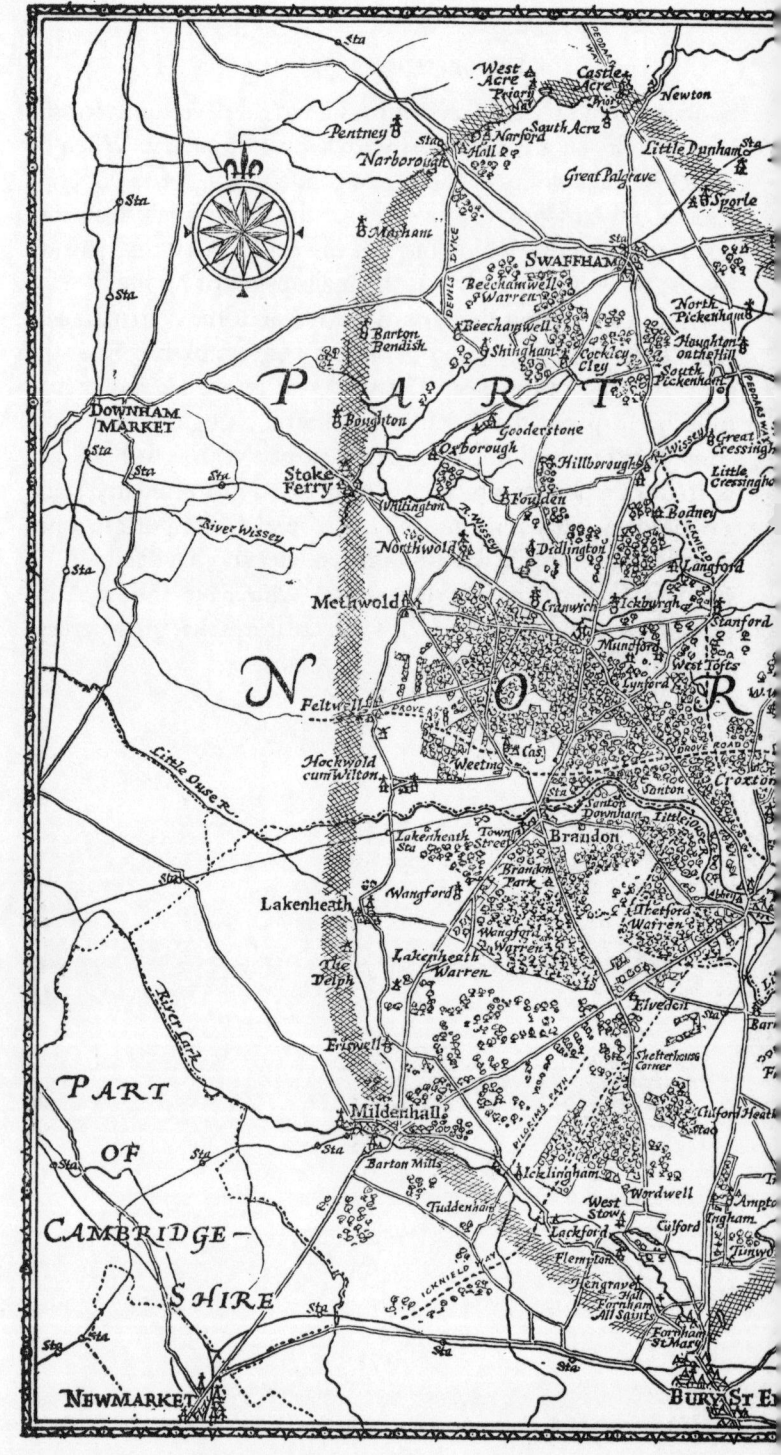

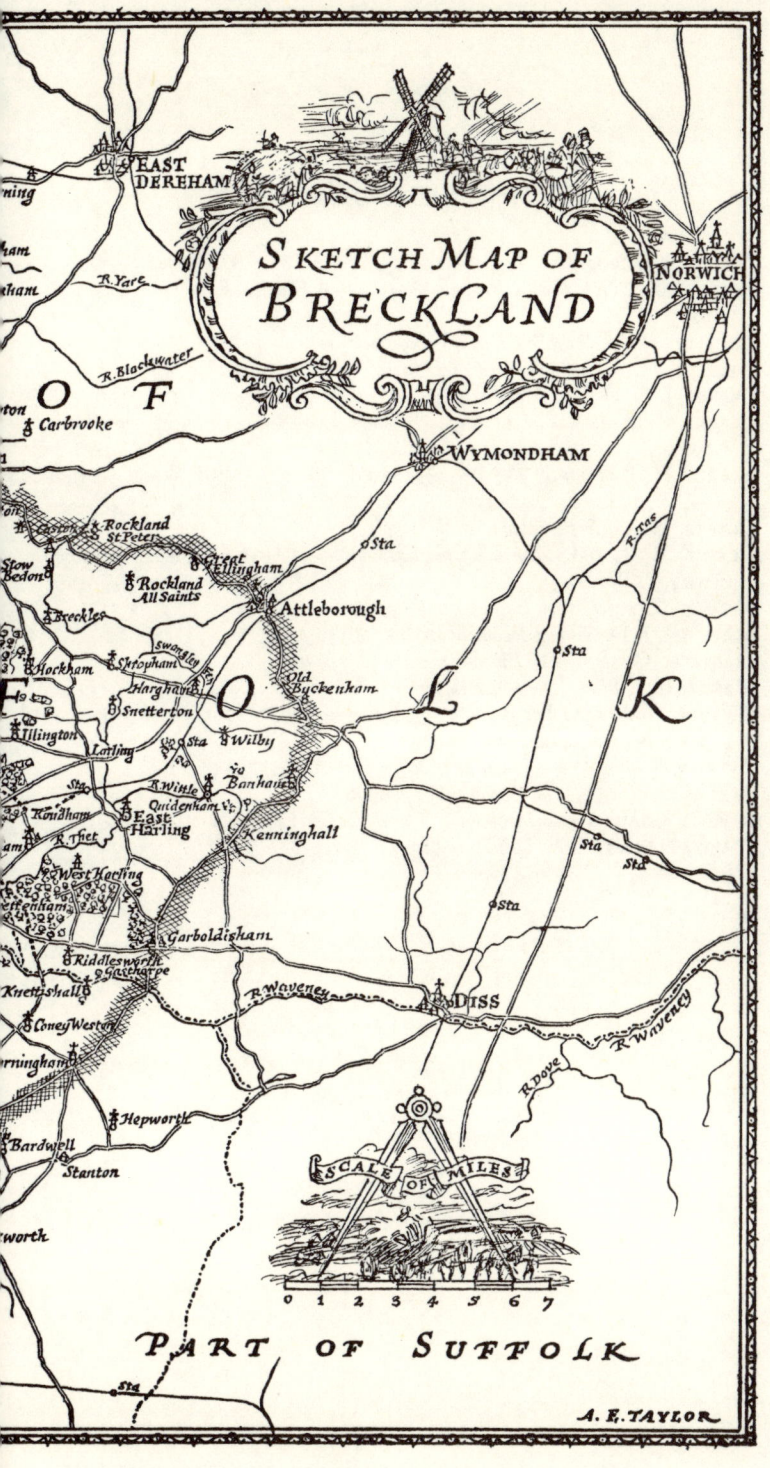

SKETCH MAP OF
BRECKLAND

EAST DEREHAM

NORWICH

R.Yare

R.Blackwater

OF

Carbrooke

WYMONDHAM

o Sta

R.Tas

Rockland
St.Peter

Stow
Bedon

Rockland
All Saints

Great
Ellingham

Breckles

Attleborough

Hockham

Swangey

Shropham

Old
Buckenham

o Sta

Hargham

Illington

Larling

Snetterton

o Sta

Wilby

R.Thet

R.Witte

o Banham

Kenningham

o Sta

o Sta

Sta Sta

Kenningham

Quidenham

East
Harling

Kenninghall

West Harling

o Sta

Garboldisham

Riddlesworth
Garthorpe

R.Waveney

DISS

Knettishall

R.Waveney

Coney Weston

R.Dove

rningham

Hepworth

Bardwell

Stanton

SCALE OF MILES

worth

0 1 2 3 4 5 6 7

o Sta

PART OF SUFFOLK

A.E.TAYLOR

SHORT BIBLIOGRAPHY

BLOOMFIELD, ROBERT. *The Farmer's Boy; Rural Tales, Ballads and Songs.*

BRAILSFORD, J. W. *The Mildenhall Treasure—A Handbook.* British Museum, 1955.

CAUTLEY, H. M. *Suffolk Churches and Their Treasures.* 1937.

CAUTLEY, H. M. *Norfolk Churches.* 1949.

CLARKE, J. G. D. *The Mesolithic Age in Britain.* 1932.

CLARKE, R. RAINBIRD. *East Anglia, Volume IV—Ancient Peoples and Places.* 1960.

CLARKE, R. RAINBIRD. *The Iron Age in Norfolk and Suffolk.* Arch. Journal XCVI, 1940.

CLARKE, W. G. *In Breckland Wilds.* 1926.

CLARKE, W. G. (ed.) *Report on the Excavations at Grime's Graves, Weeting.* 1914.

FORESTRY COMMISSION. *East Anglian Forests.*

MARGARY, I. D. *Roman Roads in Britain.* 1955.

MARTELLI, GEORGE. *The Elveden Enterprise.* 1952.

MASON, H. J. *Flint, The Versatile Stone.* 1978.

PEVSNER, NIKOLAUS. *The Buildings of England: Suffolk.* 1961. *North West and South Norfolk.* 1962.

PIGGOTT, S. *The Neolithic Cultures of the British Isles.* 1954.

ROBINSON, BRUCE. *The Peddar's Way.* 1978.

ROGERS, GRAHAM AND HICKMAN. *The Peddar's Way.* 1974.

SCARFE, NORMAN. *The Suffolk Landscape.* 1972.

INDEX

175